Hypermedia Genes

(An Evolutionary Perspective on Concepts, Models, and Architectures)

Synthesis Lectures on Information Concepts, Retrieval, and Services

Editor
Gary Marchionini, *University of North Carolina, Chapel Hill*

Hypermedia Genes: An Evolutionary Perspective on Concepts, Models, and Architectures

Nuno M. Guimarães and Luís M. Carriço

ISBN:978-3-031-01137-5   paperback
ISBN: 978-3-031-02265-4   ebook

DOI 10.1007/978-3-031-02265-4

A Publication in the Springer series
SYNTHESIS LECTURES ON INFORMATION CONCEPTS, RETRIEVAL, AND SERVICES

Lecture #11
Series ISSN
Synthesis Lectures on Information Concepts, Retrieval, and Services
Print 1947-945X   Electronic 1947-9468

Hypermedia Genes

(An Evolutionary Perspective on Concepts, Models, and Architectures)

Nuno M. Guimarães and Luís M. Carriço
University of Lisbon

SYNTHESIS LECTURES ON INFORMATION CONCEPTS, RETRIEVAL, AND SERVICES #11

ABSTRACT

The design space of information services evolved from seminal works through a set of prototypical hypermedia systems and matured in open and widely accessible web-based systems. The original concepts of hypermedia systems are now expressed in different forms and shapes.

The first works on *hypertext* invented the term itself, laid out the foundational concept of association or link, and highlighted navigation as the core paradigm for the future information systems. The first engineered systems demonstrated architectural requirements and models and fostered the emergence of the conceptual model related with the information systems and the information design. The artifacts for interaction, navigation, and search, grew from the pioneering systems.

Multimedia added a new dimension to hypertext, and mutated the term into hypermedia. The adaptation of the primitive models and mechanisms to the space of continuous media led to a further conceptual level and to the reinvention of information design methods. Hypermedia systems also became an ideal space for collaboration and cooperative work. Information access and sharing, and group work were enabled and empowered by distributed hypermedia systems.

As with many technologies, a winning technical paradigm, in our case the World Wide Web, concentrated the design options, the architectural choices and the interaction and navigation styles. Since the late nineties, the Web became the standard framework for hypermedia systems, and integrated a large number of the initial concepts and techniques. Yet, other paths are still open.

This lecture maps a simple "genome" of hypermedia systems, based on an initial survey of primitive systems that established architectural and functional characteristics, or traits. These are analyzed and consolidated using phylogenetic analysis tools, to infer families of systems and evolution opportunities. This method may prove to be inspiring for more systematic perspectives of technological landscapes.

KEYWORDS

hypertext, hypermedia, information services, evolution

Contents

Acknowledgements

The authors would like to acknowledge the support of Gary Marchionini in the inspiration for the concept of this lecture and the guidance of Diane Cerra in making it happen. The colleagues and students of the University of Lisbon and Technical University of Lisbon that have taught and studied this and related courses in these last fifteen years are also due for a special thanks. A special word of acknowledgement goes to Pedro Antunes, Teresa Chambel, and Carlos Duarte.

Thanks to the evolutionary biologists of the Faculty of Sciences of the University of Lisbon, especially Octavio Paulo, who took the time and interest to apply his phylogenetics expertise to the world of hypertext systems and taught us how to use and think with the evolution analysis tools.

Nuno M. Guimarães and Luís M. Carriço
October 2009

Preface

The domain of interactive information systems and tools where hypertext and hypermedia have played a defining role in the last decades has been populated by a host of characters, references and systems, which have been discussed, and surveyed by many designers and developers.

The emergence of the World Wide Web has shifted the focus of the designers' attention and, as with so many other technological domains like operating systems, graphics systems, and databases, some of the relevant characteristics of these systems were left in the shadow and less evident to the students and researchers of modern information systems and services.

This lecture was conceived upon the experience on teaching hypertext and hypermedia related topics at the undergraduate and graduate level since the early 90's, the relation of those topics with the complementary domains of database systems and human computer interaction, and specific contributions of individual thesis works and collective research and development projects.

This lecture tries to shift away from a traditional survey style since those surveys are generally available to the interested reader.

The methodological shift, suggested in the title of the lecture, focuses on an evolutionary analysis in the strongest possible meaning of the word. We assumed that there are evolutionary relations between several representative systems and sought to identify those relations through well established methods of living systems studies. We expect that this methodological shift can serve as an inspiration for other technological reviews and an additional motivation for interdisciplinary reasoning and questioning.

This lecture is a tribute to a community, inspired by a small number of visionaries and nurtured by a larger number of researchers and developers in different fields of work. During all these years, we praise the enthusiasm about the design, the development and critique of the new way to author and consume intellectual productions, the way to create and share information, and the way to use computers and digital media.

Nuno M. Guimarães and Luís M. Carriço
October 2009

CHAPTER 1

Introduction

Current and future information systems and services have a pervasive and intrinsic hypertextual nature. From large scale digital libraries and document repositories to specialized interactive environments, the concept of link and association, together with the navigational paradigm, has become implicit to all kinds of users in all kinds of contexts. Hypertextual behavior is now a core characteristic of all information systems and services and, actually, of our intellectual spaces, ranging from scientific production to artistic creations.

The progress of multimedia information processing capabilities and the anticipated convergence of media and computer systems accelerated the evolution of the digital information systems and services.

We adopt *hypermedia* as a common designation for information systems and services, integrating documents and information of different physical types, supporting navigation and search in flexible formats. Today, these systems are typically distributed and accessible anytime and anywhere through networked, mobile and ubiquitous devices.

From the most popular to the most specialized system, its functionality and architecture includes a number of well established and "de facto" characteristics, or traits, which have been evolving over the last decades. Information technology seems to have this unique characteristic of having condensed multiple evolutionary steps in different domains, over a very small number of earth-years, which makes it possible for a middle-aged human observer to have directly lived the actual events that populated the technological evolutionary path.

As with many other technologies, computer-based or not, the evolution that led to the current information systems landscape resulted from selection and competition, widespread adoption or specialization, and obsolescence and oblivion of many of the ancient proposals. The environmental conditions for our information systems and services are not determined by natural elements but rather by technological, social, economic or market trends, and often accidents.

An evolutionary approach to current information systems and services, based on a coherent metaphor and analysis tools of living systems, can provide an inspiring and comprehensive framework for a productive understanding of the technological evolution of this particular type of systems. This understanding facilitates the organization of fundamental concepts (or traits) and the foundations for their design, and we may anticipate prospective evolution into the future. This is the interdisciplinary approach that we adopt here, not as an attempt to build scientifically proven conclusions concerning the evolution of hypermedia systems, but as a *gedanken* experiment to explore the space of our intuitions and question some of our assumptions.

Methodologically, we adopt the following approach: the first steps include a global review of original and reference systems, from which a framework of conceptual, functional and architectural traits is derived. Contemporary or "ancient" systems, popular or not so used, adopt specific sets of these traits, or elements of a phenotype[1], in a non-uniform manner.

Based on the traits' identification, we will take the risk to perform a phylogenetic analysis[2] based on those traits. The reviewed systems, be they contemporary or historical references, are the operational taxonomical units or the species representatives of our phylogeny[3]. In Chapter 8, we will come back to the analysis procedures and tools.

This metaphor and methodology has its power and its limits. The power of the approach is to provide a systematic perspective of the evolution of a given type of technology. The results of the analysis will confirm families or classes of systems that, even if already anticipated by or emerging from our technical intuition, can now be approached in a more structured way. As we will see, this kind of modeling and analysis may trigger reflections on our interpretation of the systems' characteristics.

As much as we anticipate its power, we should also warn against a number of limitations in this style of reasoning. First, creative concepts and design decisions are not exactly characteristics, traits as we call them, determined by a genetic code. The identification of these traits and the associations between the systems and the traits is a process of interpretation, which is not universal and is definitely dependent on the authors' experience. Second, the assumption that all systems derive from a common ancestor, an assumption similar to the Tree of Life mentioned above, should not apply strictly in technological systems. These results are from multiple contributions and other times by historical, societal and economic accidents or incidents. In the case of the family of hypertext and hypermedia systems, we are lucky to have a universally accepted common ancestor, *Memex*, Vannevar Bush's conceptualized system that was ahead of the technical possibilities of its time.

1.1 THE STRUCTURE OF THIS LECTURE

This lecture opens with a chapter on the original visions and their concepts. As we will mention, current hypermedia systems and services are founded on a number of deep and primitive concepts

---

[1]Phenotype: all the observable characteristics of an organism, such as shape, size, color, and behavior that result from the interaction of its genotype (total genetic inheritance) with the environment. The common type of a group of physically similar organisms is sometimes also known as the phenotype. (Encyclopedia Britannica.) Related with Genotype: the genetic constitution of an organism. The genotype determines the hereditary potentials and limitations of an individual from embryonic formation through adulthood. From Encyclopedia Britannica, www.britannica.com

[2][www.mathworks.com > Support > Documentation > Bioinformatics Toolbox > Phylogenetic Analysis], Phylogenetic analysis is the process you use to determine the evolutionary relationships between organisms. The results of an analysis can be drawn in a hierarchical diagram called a cladogram or phylogram (phylogenetic tree). The branches in a tree are based on the hypothesized evolutionary relationships (phylogeny) between organisms. Each member in a branch, also known as a monophyletic group, is assumed to be descended from a common ancestor. Originally, phylogenetic trees were created using morphology, but now, determining evolutionary relationships includes matching patterns in nucleic acid and protein sequences.

[3]Biologists estimate that there are about 5 to 100 million species of organisms living on Earth today. Evidence from morphological, biochemical, and gene sequence data suggests that all organisms on Earth are genetically related, and the genealogical relationships of living things can be represented by a vast evolutionary tree, the Tree of Life. The Tree of Life then represents the phylogeny of organisms, i.e., the history of organism lineages as they change through time. It implies that different species arise from previous forms via descent, and that all organisms, from the smallest microbe to the largest plants and vertebrates, are connected by the passage of genes along the branches of the phylogenetic tree that links all of Life. http://tolweb.org/tree/learn/concepts/whatisphylogeny.html.

that should be defined as a meta-framework for this (and other) types of systems. The following chapter, entitled "Steps in the Evolution," is a path through a limited, but representative, set of systems that *lived* from the 70's to the early 90's. From the very early ones to a group of later research and industrial systems, a framework of hypermedia concepts, designs, data models, architectures and interaction styles has matured. The collaborative and multimedia dimensions were also evolutionary trends in many of these systems and developed strongly during this period.

The structured, document-based approach was a significant alternative to the technical design of hypermedia systems. The World Wide Web, developed at CERN and presented to the scientific and technical community in December 1991 (ACM Hypertext Conference, San Antonio, Texas), adopted from the start this approach (previously suggested in the Xanadu^{TM} system). From there, it evolved and thus guided the basic technical design and architecture of the current and pervasive information systems and services. This perspective is the subject of Section 4.

After these reviews, we will build a systematic framework of traits, or characters that cover the basic information modeling concepts, the architectural principles, design solutions and some functional options. These traits are the hypermedia genes that we see currently present in most interactive hypermedia systems and services.

After the conceptual and technological review, we carry out a phylogenetic analysis on a sample set of hypermedia systems based on the designed framework of traits. This analysis will allow us to conclude on the fundamental relations and associations between hypermedia systems. The phylogenetic analysis described in Chapter 8 uses standard tools from Evolutionary Biology studies. Some of these tools are public domain software, so we expect this analysis to be easily replicable by any interested reader.

1.2 NOT ADDRESSED HERE

As with any real world entity, hypermedia systems and services have evolved from a primordial conceptual framework and, from then on, real life conditions and stimuli have influenced the design and development of complementary functionalities. In addition, the widespread use of hypermedia systems as intellectual artifacts has opened a range of intellectual inquiries in diverse fields of knowledge.

Information search or data mining has become a major area of scientific research, technological development and product creation, as well as economic impact. The field of search engines like `www.{Google|Yahoo|Bing}.com` has grown hand in hand with the development of the current hypermedia information services. Although inseparable, when we look at the user functionality of current systems, we do not want to consider these systems at the roots of the hypermedia nature, and we do not discuss the models and techniques in this lecture. We must recognize, however, that the power of search engines emerges from the existence of a globally, interconnected network of information systems was born from the hypertextual linking mechanisms provided by the World Wide Web.

The design methodologies of hypermedia information systems, analogous to the software design methodologies, are also the subject of a large body of scientific work. These methodologies are critical to the design of the large scale information systems we use today, and we must rely on the compatibility between the design conceptual models, actual system models, and implementations (data models, presentation models, navigation models, and collaboration models). This body of knowledge, led by a persistent group of researchers for almost twenty years must be considered as an important dimension of hypermedia systems and services (Garzotto et al., 1991, 1993; Schwabe, D. and Rossi, G., 1995; Garzotto et al., 1995; Schwabe et al., 1996; Rossi et al., 1999; Sauer, S. and Engels, G., 2001; Bolchini et al., 2008). In this lecture, we take this work as an upstream condition for the construction of any hypermedia information system.

Hypertextual or hypermedia information systems and services are, as we mentioned above, intellectual tools that have a strong impact in many cognitive processes of individual human users, groups, or communities. The use and exploitation of the hypermedia information systems and services has changed, and will continue to change, the way we grasp our world in the news, the way we produce, share and acquire knowledge, the way we communicate, and the way we produce aesthetically innovative creations. Since the early days, the field of hypermedia has included a stream of reflections and theory on the new rhetorical opportunities, the new ways of writing and reading, and the application of these systems to practical fields of work as an augmentation tool for our intellectual and creative capacity. While this feature may be the ultimate meaning of life for hypermedia systems, we leave it aside as the ultimate inquiry (Delany, P. and Landow, G.P., 1991; Landow, G.P., 1987, 1994; Bernstein, M., 1999; Bolter, J.D., 1991; Moulthrop, S., 1991, 1992; Bolter, J.D. and Grusin, R., 2000; Kaplan, N. and Moulthrop, S., 1994; Joyce et al., 1989).

1.3 HOW TO USE THIS LECTURE

The end goal of this lecture is to review a set of key reference systems and associated concepts, which have shaped the design of current information systems and services, and conclude on the evolutionary relations between those systems and concepts.

The lecture has the structure mentioned above and is backed by a large number of bibliographic references. We looked for authoritative and easily reachable references. Most of the references are included in the ACM (Association for Computing Machinery) digital library. ACM initiatives (Conferences, workshops, and publications) have had a crucial impact in the development of this field (or fields). Moreover, the ACM digital library, as many other publishers of the references included in this lecture, adopts the DOI addressing scheme, meaning that most referred papers are directly available (provided that the required subscriptions are valid) from the reference lists. Books, of course, may not be available so easily, but all the referred books have been noted with ISBN-13 identifiers. A small number of resources are directly accessible through WWW URL's, but we tended to refer to standard and stable organizations (like the World Wide Web Consortium W3C).

This network of references lets us believe that this lecture can be useful for the interested student as a good source of reference information and as an example, specially, given the final experiments, for news ways to approach technology evolution.

The choice of the set of systems under analysis is debatable. We believe that the chosen ones are individually unquestionable, not only for their complete design and for proven technical effectiveness, but due to the conceptual impact in design and architecture of future systems. Some commercial systems were left out of this analysis due to their similarity to the included ones. The differences between Web-based systems (browsers, variations in the scripting languages) were not considered as sufficiently rich discriminators for design and conceptual purposes. Some successors or evolutions of some of the mentioned systems (like *Dolphin* versus *Sepia*, or *Aquanet* versus *NoteCards*) were referred but not as individual systems, so not to focus on too segmented aspects of hypermedia systems. For the purpose of the analysis, be it the definition of the traits framework or the evolutionary analysis, the limited set of sample systems was considered appropriate since the addition of more exemplar systems or the explosion of traits would not improve the robustness of our discussion and possible conclusions.

CHAPTER 2

Original Visions and Concepts

The background of current and future information systems and services has its roots deep in seminal visions related with thinking, reasoning and knowing, and with the projection of these human capacities into design proposals. Broadly taken, today's hypertext and multimedia information systems assume the role of intellectual technologies; insofar, they adapt and couple with our human thought and creative processes.

The reasoning that led, and will continue to lead, to the view of technical systems as intellectual artifacts is a classical question with a long and ancient tradition, and this way of thinking was recently reborn with the emergence and development of information technologies (Lévy, P., 1990). We need not go as far as the invention of writing (Lerner, F., 1998; Robinson, A., 1995) or the printing press (Eisenstein, E.L., 1980), but the breakthrough reflection in the domain of information or knowledge systems has been presented and established by Vannevar Bush in his widely known and discussed paper "As We May Think" (Bush, V., 1945; Simpson et al., 1996).

2.1   KNOWLEDGE AND ASSOCIATION

The conceptual underpinnings of Bush's vision were the notion of a technological system as a shared repository of knowledge, coupled with the concept of *association* as the fundamental mechanism of human thinking, an idea born in the Western philosophical and psychological traditions (Rapaport, D., 1974). This vision, outlined in 1945, was strongly inspired by a massive exposure to knowledge creation (the scientific campaign of the Second World War).

A knowledge repository and an interaction style that matches the human cognitive mechanisms are the primary elements of any intellectual technology and artifact, and they are deep genes of any modern hypermedia information system.

Bush outlined the requirement of the matching between the interaction style and the cognitive activity under the topic of "selection speed" or "readiness." Later reflections on the design of computer-based artifacts (Winograd, T. and Flores, F., 1986) created consolidated theoretical views on this requirement.

To this conceptual background, Bush added a prospective realization of the Memex system and futuristic anticipations concerning technical functionality, and media integration. Furthermore, Bush added user profiles and skills that only today are becoming a reality (generalized digital photography, compression and storage, effective speech recognition, and *trailblazing* as a specialized professional activity).

2.2   NON-LINEARITY AND NAVIGATION

The associative nature of an interactive knowledge repository is directly related with the notion of non-linearity. While the concept and use of non-linearity in texts and information sources can be traced back to the origins of writing and followed up along literary traditions and families, the support for association, or linking, as a fundamental design principle brought the non-linearity of the "text" to the forefront of the conceptual framework of hypermedia systems.

The term "hypertext," which invention is attributed to Ted Nelson, as defined and discussed in *Literary Machines* (Nelson, T.H., 1980), was the definite expression of the non-linear or non-sequential nature of the new information systems. This idealization was the critical step that radically created new opportunities and later implemented technological artifacts and mechanisms that supported non-sequential reading and writing; this was done in such a way that some good level of *structural coupling* (Maturana, H. and Varela, F., 1987) between a human user and an electronic machine could be achieved.

As an immediate corollary to non-sequential reading, navigation came up as the intrinsic interaction style with hypermedia systems. Vannevar Bush already considered the navigation style as the primordial one, and he was visionary to the point of anticipating a well defined expertise related with the task of building "trails" or "paths" throughout the network of related information elements (Bush, V., 1945).

The navigational interaction paradigm (Nielsen, J., 1990) ought to be considered as a radical change in the way information was, and can be, accessed and shared. Navigation is definitely apart from interrogation, or querying, a method that requires some minimal knowledge of the information's semantic and syntactic model. Navigation is also different from search. Search and query relies upon the actual content on the information elements and, even today, does not yet fully explore the structural role of an information element and the semantics of the linking decisions that connect that information element to the global network (Segaran et al., 2009; Antoniou, G. and van Harmelen, F., 2008).

2.3   AUGMENTATION AND SERENDIPITY

The view on knowledge creation and organization, the adoption of association as a fundamental cognitive and reasoning mechanism supported by a technological device implementing this association or link, shaped the nature of current hypermedia information systems.

From the early designs, augmentation was a key motivation for hypermedia systems. Augmentation was (and is) understood as an expansion of cognitive and intellectual capabilities. The unavoidable reference for this concept is Doug Engelbart's proposals back in the 1960's (Engelbart, D.C., 1962). In his framework, a pioneering hypertext system NLS/Augment played a determining role. The framework, HLAM/T, induced wider interpretations and is, still today, a valuable analysis tool for a systematic criticism of technological artifacts and innovations.

A less highlighted deep feature of hypermedia information systems is the notion of *serendipity*. The concept is defined in the Webster's Online Dictionary[1] as "*pure luck in discovering things you were not looking for*," or more soundly in the College Edition[2], as " *[coined (c. 1754) by Horace Walpole after The Three Princes of Serendip (i.e., Sri Lanka), a Pers fairy tale in which the princes make such discoveries] an apparent aptitude for making fortunate discoveries accidentally*." In any case, its translation to different languages seems to be a challenge to many linguists.

Serendipity seems to be the ultimate creative effect of the free association and navigation enabled by hypermedia information systems and services. As with the other deep traits, it has strong implications in the technological design and particularly on the power of hypermedia systems as intellectual augmentation tools. Umberto Eco in Serendipities (Eco, U., 1998) delightfully highlights the effect and implications of serendipity in intellectual traditions and cultural history. It is also a dear concept to the scientific enterprise, with a personal flavor to us, authors of this lecture, and members of a community with a long historical tradition of exploration and discovery in the sense of Daniel Boorstin (Boorstin, D.J., 1985).

In summary, as a first step into the feature classification of hypermedia information systems and services, we retain this small set of deep characteristics, common to all the individual systems that we want to consider in the context of this lecture:

- Knowledge and association,

- Non-linearity and navigation,

- Augmentation and serendipity.

---

[1] Webster's Online Dictionary, http://www.websters-online-dictionary.org.
[2] Third College Edition of Webster's New World Dictionary of American English, Victoria Neufeldt (ed.) and David B. Guralink (ed), Webster's New World, Prentice Hall, 1988.

CHAPTER 3

Steps in the Evolution

Each one of the hypermedia systems we used as a reference proposed a set of complete and fully functional features. Due to common inspiration and mutual influence, these systems bootstrapped the development of a set of traits. At this stage, we will separate these traits into five main classes where characteristics that are more detailed will fit in as we go along. The traits are organized in the following classes:

(a) Link and association typology,

(b) Interaction styles and support,

(c) Data models and information structure,

(d) Architecture and scale,

(e) Design and functional goals.

Link and association typology specifically refers to the types of nodes and links that materialize the association concept and their structure. *Interaction and presentation styles* are associated with the former linking mechanisms but define the representation of the links and nodes in the context of the interaction, and they introduce the basic elements of navigational rhetoric. *Data models and information structure* define the structural principles that guide the organization of information from a data storage and sharing perspective, independently, from the presentation choices. *Architecture and scale* are engineering options that were adopted, implicitly or explicitly, by each individual system and have constrained the system development and use in one or other way. *Design and functional goals* is a broader dimension, to be called upon when systems have a targeted functional scope and a corresponding design.

3.1 ORIGINAL SYSTEMS

After the seminal concepts have been laid by Bush and Engelbart, a initial group of systems made its presentation. Incurring the risk of presenting a biased interpretation of this pioneering nature, systems like HES (Hypertext Editing System)/FRESS (File Retrieval and Editing System) (Durand, D.G. and DeRose, S.J., 1993; Meyrowitz, N. and van Dam, A., 1982), NLS (oN Line System)/Augment (Engelbart, D., 1968a, 1988a), and Xanadu (Nelson, T.H., 1999) are widely accepted as the very first group of hypertext creations.

This initial group of systems influenced a lot of the functionality of the successor hypertext and hypermedia systems, and they were, in fact, key contributors to basic characteristics of interactive computing (the invention of the "mouse" by Doug Engelbart or graphics screens with windows, as in NLS or FRESS, the text formatting and printing of HES). The purpose of the lecture is not to provide an exhaustive review of the historical representatives of hypertext systems but rather to grasp an evolution path based on an incremental identification of traits.

The **NLS/Augment** system introduced a number of defining features of hypermedia systems in the 1960's (Engelbart, D., 1968a; Engelbart, D. and English, W., 1968b; Engelbart, D., 1988a,b; Engelbart, D. and Nelson, T., 1995), and it became, most probably, the reference for the technological feasibility, as much as Memex has become the conceptual one. The demonstration of NLS/Augment, back in 1968 (see Fig. 3.1), is now available in video through multiple Internet services, and can still be taken as a reference for interactive functionality as well as a rational for the design of "intellectual augmentation" environments.

Figure 3.1: A snapshot of the 1968 demonstration of NLS/Augment, (Engelbart, D., 1968a).

We should highlight the following features: the notion of the information space as a hierarchical system of structured documents, explicitly organized in nodes, already assumed to include text, graphics or even digitized voice; the notion of links as first-order objects, addressable and typed, and, therefore, stored independently from the documents; and the notion of multiple views of the information based on various criteria.

Xanadu[TM] can be considered a peer of NLS/Augment in this seminal role of pioneering the creation of a conceptual space for hypermedia systems. One of the paramount references, *Literary Machines* (Nelson, T.H., 1980), first edition appearing in 1980, describes most of the proposed features. Beyond the presentation of the foundational concept, the term *hypertext* itself, *Literary Machines* (LM) goes on in the enumeration of the specific features of a hypertext system. In particular, the following are important:

- The discussion of the "linking" system (LM, Sec. 2.4) where the possible types of links are anticipated: links as jump opportunities with a return option, commentaries, bookmarks, and marginal notes (virtual yellow stickers). Links are assumed to be typed, directional, and associate spans (a *from-set* and a *to-set*) of heterogeneous data types. A large set of link types is already proposed by Literary Machines: metalinks applicable to whole documents and similar to current metadata (title, version); ordinary text links, for sequential documents and similar to document structure tags (correction, comment, translation, heading, paragraph, quote, footnote); hypertext links as we would expect (jumps, modal jumps, thread suggestions, expansion); and literary links, immersed in the *docuverse* (citation, alternative version, comment, certification, mail).

- The concept of transclusion (Nelson, T.H., 1995) encompasses and encapsulates a group of finer-grained concepts. Transclusion can be defined as "inclusion by reference," as opposed to an inclusion by value[1] (thus implying copy of the included source into the referent destination). Transclusion assumes that data elements exist in a unique and single version in the universal document space, *docuverse*, and, when pointed to by links in any document, get a representation in the particular context of the reference.

- The presentation of a link is considered a "front-end issue," thus separating content/data from presentation/interaction. The function of the front-end (nowadays, globally known as *browser*) was defined to be presentation and manipulation.

- The main unit of the information space is a document with an associated owner and a set of outgoing links (incoming links are inside other documents). Document composition is defined as a limitless "windowing" mechanism whereby documents can include others of different owners and sources. This structure opened the discussion on the storage gains and avoidance of distributed update needs. Versioning (and historical backtrack) was proposed as an important mechanism for document organization.

- Once the basic structure was defined, the open publishing requirements came up, namely issues of copyright and royalties. We should realize that these are still open themes in the status of the technology. The proposal of Xanadu[TM] was based on the idea that, given that, any document has an owner, and everything is a document in the system. The presentation of a document to

---

[1]Not very far from the analogous duality in programming languages (function parameters passed by reference or by value).

a user would trigger a distribution of royalties to the set of owners of the documents presented to that user in some proportional way.

- Literary Machines foresaw the "disadvantages," or the practical impossibility, of having a central server for the universal publishing network. Therefore, a distributed and networked architecture of the system was planned to support the *docuverse*. An addressing scheme for units within the system was then proposed. Moreover, the Front-End/Back-End (or client-server) communication should be based on a specific FEBE protocol (FEBE 87.1 specified in BNF), supporting a set of operations (*retrieval, insertion, deletion, copy, rearrange, makelink, findlink*, etc.). Another proposed concept was the BEBE protocol (Back End to Back End) as a unification mechanism for multiple Xanadu™ servers.

Even if the actual Xanadu™ system has not met their designer's expectations, as a widely available and used system, the rich set of concepts has paved the way to much of what we witness today as the digital information publishing space[2].

3.2   REFERENCE SYSTEMS

After the above pioneering systems, the design, implementation and user experience grew systems all over the technological landscape. We will not describe these systems' functionalities in detail, which would be redundant to the large body of literature, be it the original scientific references we include here or historical retrospectives of the past systems. We intend, however, to gather, with the short notes presented below, a set of defining traits of a particular generation of systems, the pre-world-wide-web systems, that were mostly designed and presented in the second half of the eighties, and the first years of the nineties[3].

Hypercard (Harvey, G., 1988; Michel, S.L., 1988; Natchez, M. and Prose, T., 1989) was a famous pioneering system, either considered as an hypertext system, an application building environment, or a data base design tool. Distributed with every Apple Macintosh computer, it became a central reference for hypertext concepts and functionalities, and it is still considered by many as the definite contributor to the development of hypertext literacy among the common computer user.

The main **Hypercard** metaphor was the pile of cards, a basic node construct. A Hypercard document or application (depending on your perspective) is a collection of cards, in other words, a

---

[2]The presentation of the Xanadu System in Literary Machines is filled with interesting discussions and predictions. Business models and the role and caveats of digital advertising were also foreseen (such as the determination of what would actually be shown on the screen). Personal, ethical and societal issues were also raised in Literary Machines: user privacy, publishing freedom, possibility of anonymous publication, copyright protections. The projected usage costs including storage and networking costs for 1990 are presented (20 US$/Mb, 5 US$/hour of connection time in prime time, 0.01 US$/Kb or 10 US$/Mb), and an funding scheme was considered including the support to an author's fund and publication fees.

[3]The most important conferences for presentation of these early systems and design contributions were ACM Hypertext'87 (Chapel Hill, NC, USA), ACM Hypertext'89 (Pittsburgh, PA, USA), European Conference on Hypertext'90 (ECHT'90, Paris, France), ACM Hypertext'91 (San Antonio, TX, USA) and ACM Hypertext'92 (Milano, Italy). The World Wide Web was demonstrated in San Antonio, TX, in 1991 and the first reference to WWW in the index of these Hypertext Conference Proceedings appears in ECHT'94 (European Conference on Hypertext, ACM, Edinburgh, UK, 1994). The conference series is still very active today, and the 20th ACM Hypertext Conference took place in June'2009, in Torino, Italy.

stack. Each card had a fixed sized and was presented individually in the screen. Cards had an internal structure including a background (shareable among several cards). Backgrounds or individual cards can integrate different types of objects such as graphical elements, buttons, and text fields. Each card/node has a set of attributes open to modification through specific dialogues. These attributes configure the basic operations like browsing, text input, drawing, authoring or object creation and program creation (scripting). All these attributes are thus defined to control the interaction style and behavior of any object.

A central feature of HyperCard was its **scripting language** called HyperTalk, which clearly influenced future systems to incorporate this capacity. Any object from the Stack of Cards to any individual Button could have an associated script, or a small interpreted program, which would be activated in a set of given conditions (when displayed, when selected, or when a numerical expression became true). HyperTalk was a simple interpreted language inspired in BASIC or Smalltalk.

Links in Hypercard were implemented as HyperTalk scripts and were, therefore, intrinsically **dynamic**, operating in the limited and constrained name space of a Card's stack but also capable of executing simple graphical and interactive operations. Implicitly, the Hypercard link embeds the basic mechanism for an extended notion of link, known as multi-point links (or "fat links"). **Search and query** (within the limited information space of each Hypercard stack) was also included as a base functionality.

KMS (Akscyn et al., 1987, 1988; Yoder et al., 1989), designed as an industrially-targeted **distributed hypertext** environment (preceded by CMU's ZOG (McCracken, D.L. and Akscyn, R.M., 1984), emphasized some fundamental engineering characteristics, namely an explicit concern for performance ("no more than one second to follow a link") as a critical interaction requirement and a clear option against overlapping windows as a presentation design principle[4].

Any item in a frame (or node) could be defined as a source of a link (**anchor**) and these connections, once established in a typically, hierarchical structure of nodes, were explicitly signaled and represented by graphic conventions (a @ prefix). Navigation was implicitly aided through this induced information model.

KMS has also integrated a dedicated **scripting language**, which scripts could be associated to any element in the frames, and activated according to a user's decision.

Hyperties   (Koved, L. and Shneiderman, B.,   1986;   Shneiderman, B.,   1987; Shneiderman, B., Ed., 1988b; Shneiderman, B., 1989) (originally named as TIES – The Interactive Electronic Encyclopedia) was designed and developed in the University of Maryland by Ben Shneiderman's team, beginning in the early eighties. The human factors, user interface design, and engineering culture of the group (Shneiderman, B., 1988a) was a determining factor in the design of the system. HyperTIES proposed simple solutions for links (reference links or simple point-to-node links) but pioneered the simplification of the link presentation. The use of highlighted or colored text, currently, the universal understanding of a link in the Web based

---

[4]The CMU's Andrew Windows System, contemporary to KMS/ZOG, and a competitor of the MIT's X-Windows System, followed a similar principle – tiled windows instead of overlapping windows (Neuwirth, C. and Ogura, A., 1988; Sherman et al., 1990; Palay, A.J., et al, 1988).

systems, was proposed by HyperTIES, moving away from special characters or symbols, menus or buttons. The system adopted a simple node/page paradigm and created, analyzed or refined fundamental concepts in current information systems such as the *history* tool, the *back* button, and the *image map* solution for linking from graphical representations.

HyperTies had already considered the information structuring tools and the programming capability. Actually, the system included a markup language, HTML, standing at the time for HyperTIES Markup Language and a simple script language to associate computational processes with pages or links.

Guide (Brown, P., 1987, 1992, 1994) was one of the first systems to bet on large scale adoption and generalized commercial promotion of a hypertext system. From the University of Kent at Canterbury, UK, to OWL International Ltd (Office Workstation Ltd), Guide has highlighted a number of concepts related with the design for usability of the information structure and content. The system discussed and proposed a minimal set of presentation modalities, centered around the notion of a single scrollable page, together with different types of buttons, or links: replacement-buttons (that lead to another block of text when selected), note-buttons associated with the creation of a separate interaction space (window), and reference buttons (closer to simple links).

Guide has also integrated a "*find*" functionality, something that was considered in the early days of hypertext as a heterodox design option, as the Guide designers themselves recognized since navigation should be privileged with respect to search and query.

NoteCards (Trigg et al., 1986; Halasz et al., 1987) developed at Xerox PARC, CA, USA, on the workstation Interlisp environment, adopted a simple model based on simple (typed) nodes (NoteCards) and links. From the start, it considered basic composition constructs (nested fileboxes) and **navigation-oriented structures** (browsers consisting of structure diagrams of the network). Links were simple directional pairs of source-destination node, but the idea of **typed links** was a key element of the NoteCards proposal. The link typing principle (together with a representation of this type through a label in the link) supported the original goal of building semantic networks.

While not initially implemented in NoteCards, the system designers laid out (Halasz, F.G., 1988) a number of requirements for the future hypertext and publishing systems, which are relevant in the context of this lecture. We will not attribute them to the original NoteCards system, but we will consider them in the evolutionary framework we are looking for: (a) the rationale and relevance of integrating search and query facilities in the hypermedia system; (b) the design and development of rich hypermedia data models where the composition principles should be taken one step further; (c) interaction facilities to support structure creation (virtual structures); (d) active computation in the hypermedia system to support more autonomous evolution of the hypermedia network; (e) versioning of nodes and links; (f) support for collaborative work, (g) extensibility and tailorability.

With NoteCards, its application environment and its designers at Xerox PARC were also responsible for a strong push on the design of **navigation support mechanisms**, namely Paths/Scripted Documents (Zellweger, P.T., 1989; Furuta et al., 1997) or Guided Tours (Marshall, C.C. and Irish, P.M., 1989).

Intermedia was another determining system for the evolution of the hypermedia technology as we know it today. Intermedia was designed, developed and intensively used at the Brown University (Meyrowitz, N., 1986; Yankelovitch et al., 1989; Kahn et al., 1990; Haan et al., 1992). The key traits we should emphasize here are as follows:

- The **generalization of the anchor** notion as a persistent selection in multiple media, which implied and was also a consequence of the integration of different types of editors considered useful and relevant for the construction of complex hypermedia documents or structures (InterWord for textual documents, InterMail for mail messages, InterVal for timelines, InterVideo for digital video, InterDraw for graphics and InterPlay for animated sequences).

- The connections between anchors, the actual **links**, were considered **as first class objects**, and they were kept in a dedicated link server, and supported in some generic database management system. This separation of data and linking information was considered a basic requirement for flexibility and support to collaboration (Catlin et al., 1989).

- The design of **visual support for navigation** that was considered in complex hypermedia structures. Intermedia has stressed, as other contemporary systems the importance of supporting navigation with graph-like representations of the information structure.

- The collaborative dimension that was considered in the early design stages and then explicitly in the design and critique of **collaborative annotation** support.

3.3   DATA MODELS

From the early design proposals and implementation reports, a concern for a structured and systematic definition of a hypertextual data model emerged, together with a clearer and clearer view of the content storage system's requirements and desired functionality (Stotts, P. and Furuta, R., 1989; Tompa, F., 1989; Oliveira et al., 2001).

The notion of composition in the data model was adopted from the very early systems. **HAM** (Campbell, B. and Goodman, J., 1988), or Hypertext Abstract Machine, proposed a first concept for composition, designated as *Context*, which allowed for the construction of a hierarchical tree based on a simple parent-child relationship, with the *Graph* as the overall container. Apart from this basic composition mechanism, the HAM data model was still a minimalist one, including the additional concepts of *Nodes*, *Links* and *Attributes* (attached to any one of the previous entities).

In 1990, the central contribution to the evolution of the hypertext data models and associated storage services was the proposal of the **Dexter Hypertext Reference Model** (DHRM) (Halasz, F. and Schwartz, M., 1994; Leggett, J.J. and Schnase, J.L., 1994; Grønbæk, K., 1994; Grønbæk, K. and Trigg, R.H., 1994a; Grønbæk, K., and Trigg, R.H., 1994b; Grønbæk, K. and Trigg, R.H., 1996; Grønbæk et al., 1997; Dodd, R., 2008) in the context of a Hypertext Standardization Workshop. The context for this proposal was a growing proliferation of hypertext systems, such as the ones we reviewed above, and an expectation for new ones. This scenario suggested a convergence in interchange and interoperability standards. That was the main goal of the Dexter Model, an "*attempt to capture, both formally and informally, the important abstractions found in a wide range of existing and future hypertext systems.*"

The DHRM proposed a three-layer model separating *storage*, *runtime* support and *within-component*, with a stronger focus on the first one, thus reinforcing the importance of the data modeling component. The definition of a *Component* concept, supporting hierarchical organization, together with *Links*, was the base of the storage model. The *within-component* layer, not elaborated by the DHRM, should be concerned with the specifics of the contents within each component. The relevant concern of DHRM was the *anchoring* mechanism that should support the link typologies mentioned above, and which constitutes the interface between the *storage layer* and the *within-component* layer. Reciprocally, the *runtime* layer was underspecified by the DHRM to allow for multiple solutions on the presentation of content and links. The model defined an interface between *storage* and *runtime* layers as a *presentation specification*.

On the data model itself, the DHRM defined an address space (UID's, or unique identifiers, for components), mechanisms for indirect addressing (resolver and accessor functions), anchors (within components) and links, associating components/anchors and specifying directionality.

Later in 1993 (Hardman, L., et al, 1993), the new scenarios created by the dissemination of multimedia systems, based on digital video and audio, led to the design of the **Amsterdam Hypermedia Model** (AHM). The concepts proposed by DHRM have then been extended to support both spatial and temporal information, and the linking/anchoring mechanisms evolved to encompass the notion of *synchronization*, a key aspect that is required to integrate content with dynamic media. AHM has been designed in the confluence of the DHRM and CMIF (CWI Multimedia Interchange Format), and it has demonstrated its capacity to support systems and specifications like Intermedia, Guide, Microcosm or even HTML definitions but also multimedia environments like Athena Muse (Hodges et al., 1989), other systems already coined as hypermedia and language-based constructs like HyTime (Newcomb et al., 1991; Buford, J.F., 1996) or SMIL (Synchronized Multimedia Integration Language) (Bulterman, D., 2001), which became later generalized as hypermedia specification languages in Web-based information services.

The multimedia evolution was definitely based on the previously consolidated views of the Dexter Hypertext Reference Model (Garzotto et al., 1994).

3.4   OPEN HYPERMEDIA ARCHITECTURES

Closely related with the work on data models, information system and services based on the hypermedia principles have developed architectural models and construction principles that led to the contemporary engineering solutions. The central notion of "open hypermedia systems" (OHS) (Wiil et al., 1996; Haake, A. and Hicks, D., 1997; Akscyn, R. and McCracken, D., 1993; Nuernberg et al., 1998) reflects the option of separating content data and hypertextual structure from interaction and presentation, a design option already implicit in the models that we described above.

In 1989, one of the first expressions of open hypermedia systems was the proposal of the **Sun's Link Service** (Pearl, A., 1989). The aim of breaking the traditional monolithic structure of hypermedia systems was central to the proposal of a "link database" and "link service." From this architectural decision, the service addressed the issues of open hypertext environments, notably link maintenance, versioning and relation with the presentation layers. The communication between client applications and the link service was ruled by a specific protocol. This protocol required the registration of the application in the service, and, therefore, assumed the existence of a "session" layer. As we will see, the concept of a session-based or stateful protocol, as opposed to a stateless protocol, is a critical decision in the architecture of hypermedia environments that are required to be scalable, and this has clearly had an impact in the design decisions of the World Wide Web developers.

The definition of the architectural concept of Hyperbase developed quickly. In the Hypertext conference stream, the architecture of **SEPIA** (Schütt, H.A. and Streitz, N.A., 1990; Streitz et al., 1993) was presented with an emphasis of its storage component, *HyperBase*. The goals and approach were clearly to design and build an application independent storage system, based on an application-independent data model, including an appropriate query language and supporting concurrency control. *HyperBase* was built on top of a standard relational database and also showed how the hypertext and object oriented data model could be specified and implemented as a layer on top of a less structured and generic DBMS.

Microcosm (Fountain et al., 1990; Davis et al., 1992; Hill, G. and Hall, W., 1994; Davis, H.C., 1999) proposed an analogous architecture with solutions to support application independent links and leading to a *"generalized multimedia information management environment."* The requirements advocated the needs of an adaptable environment for data, tools and service integration, independence from the computing platform, support for information search, update, annotation and exchange, as well as media independent with respect to the conceptual functionalities. In Microcosm, links are of different types (specific, local and generic), supporting traditional point-to-point links and document-to-document links but also dynamically computed links. Conceptual data independence and integration with the *document control system* is achieved through a set of viewers with different degrees of Microcosm-awareness (full, partial or none).

Hyper-G (Andrews et al., 1995a,b; Maurer, H., 1995) is a open hypermedia system designed at the Technical University of Graz, Austria, in the early 90's. It supported a number of features that could be considered as alternatives to the World-Wide-Web proposals. Hyper-G has assumed interoperability with Web servers and integration of Web browsers (*Mosaic,* in the beginning of times, back in the early 90's).

The Hyper-G document model is a complex one (document clusters) supporting multiple views of a document. Documents are included in collections and collections are organized hierarchically. Collections are actually Hyper-G databases to which users can connect from any location. Search within the scope of collections is provided. The definition of mechanisms to support a structured large-scale information space was, therefore, one of the main goals of Hyper-G. In addition, the annotation facilities and the authorization and rights management functionalities included in the main design were targeted at the development of collaborative work scenarios.

Hyper-G has approached the typology of links in a particular way, extending the standard notions of the Web environments. Hyper-G supported bidirectional links, thus including the standard point-to-point forward link but also the reciprocal back-link. Back-links are a critical mechanism to support information integrity and coherence, in spite of the constraints on the management of scalability that the concept implies. Links in Hyper-G are typed, supporting both the creation of a semantic structure in the documents (e.g., link types like "definition," "abstract," "illustration"), and the creation of cooperative processes based on particular types of roles ("comments, annotation," "review"). Moreover, links in Hyper-G are stored separately and can be filtered on an individual (e.g., links of type "annotation") or group basis (e.g., all the links of a document). Hyper-G has proposed graphical representations of the document structure, including 3-D versions[5].

The Hyper-G technology and experience eventually evolved to a commercial product and company, HyperWave[6]. In 2009, HyperWave solutions are presented as a Content Management System, complemented with e-learning and collaborative functionalities.

The conceptual background of Hyper-G is strongly influenced by Xanadu™, and still today, the concept of transclusion is present in the scientific group directly associated with the Hyper-G origins (Krottmaier, H., 2002).

3.5   COMPONENT-BASED APPLICATIONS

The architectural guidelines are also relevant in the design and programming frameworks of hypermedia applications, more typically clients, if we assume generalized client-server architecture for hypermedia systems.

The software architecture of hypermedia applications was strongly influenced and developed together with the emergence of the object oriented programming technology (during the 80's). Object oriented technologies tend to have a perfect fit with the hypermedia conceptual space, fertile in needs for encapsulation, generalization and specialization of heterogeneities, in data models, data types, and relations between classes and objects.

The objective of integrating encapsulated and generic hypermedia components in general purpose applications was outlined in (Meyrowitz, N., 1986). The design of a generic set of hypermedia components could support the integration of this hypermedia functionality without explicit concern for the storage and retrieval mechanisms or the details of the representation/visualization systems (Puttress, J. and Guimarães, N., 1990). The genericity of the components was based on the abstraction support provided by the programming languages (Guimarães, N., 1991).

---

[5]Interesting to see the relations between these representations and current prototypes/demonstrations distributed by project Xanadu, www.xanadu.net, for 3D representation of hypertextual structures (XANADU™ 1.0).
[6]www.hyperwave.com.

The dissemination of the Web browsers with the integration of the Java engines (or runtime environments) opened the way for a richer integration of active components in hypermedia documents (see also ActiveX controls in the Microsoft broader framework). Java Applets were, at some stage, the type of components most frequently used to enhance hypermedia documents.

Current hypermedia services are adopting new types of programming support for the active components. Ajax (Holdener, A., 2008) (Asynchronous Javascript with XML) is a programming framework that gathers a number of Web-related technologies (XHTML, CSS, DOM, XML and XSLT, XMLHttpRequest and Javascript). Independent of the technical details and intricacies of blending this set of technologies, Ajax seems to be providing useful environment to develop interactive and responsive components within hypermedia documents.

3.6   GROUP AND COLLABORATIVE BEHAVIOR

Hypermedia systems have addressed, through a number of early representatives, the distributed and cooperative dimension. As we highlighted above, the very first system designs of NLS/Augment or KMS, not to mention the universal nature of Xanadu^{TM}, have assumed that hypermedia information systems and services were to be accessed and manipulated in a distributed and cooperative way. Some degree of concurrency control has always been present in these multi-user hypermedia systems, which was further taken into consideration in the architecture of the hyperbases of open hypermedia systems. The support for versioning also relates directly with the foundational support for collaborative work.

The intrinsic collaboration support provided by distributed multiuser hypermedia systems is just one of the relevant benefits of this family of systems. From the first generation of hypermedia designs, it became evident that a shared and multimedia information systems based on a flexible data model, together with interactive mechanisms for authoring and navigation was a natural platform for the development of tools to support higher level collaborative processes, like argumentation, design deliberation, collaborative writing and collective knowledge in general (Thüring et al., 1995; Wang, W. and Rada, R., 1998).

gIBIS (Conklin, J. and Begeman, M.L., 1987, 1988; Bernstein et al., 1993; Conklin et al., 2001) made a defining contribution to consolidate the nature of a family of systems, positioned in the domain of "argumentation." gIBIS was, according to the authors, "*an application specific hypertext system designed to facilitate the capture of early design deliberations. It implements a specific method, called Issue Based Information Systems (IBIS), which has been developed for use on large, complex design problems.*"

Beyond the design issues that were/are typical of hypertext spaces like navigation, search and query, or graphical representation solutions, gIBIS demonstrated the power of hypertext as an instantiation of a domain information model in an interactive environment usable by humans. This capacity of tailored hypermedia systems is strongly related with the existence of a flexible type model for information elements and relations, i.e., for nodes and links. In the case of gIBIS, the IBIS method materialized into a set of node types (*issues*, *positions* and *arguments*) and a set of link types (*generalizes* or *specializes*, *responds-to*, *questions* or *is-suggested-by*, *supports* or *objects-to*).

At the same time, and also aiming at the exploration of hypermedia systems as a particular kind of knowledge representation environments differentiated from the approaches proposed by Artificial Intelligence disciplines, the NoteCards has been used as the platform for supporting these representations. Some examples were the Rational Actor Model (Allison, G.T. and Zelikow, P., 1999) for policy decision making or the Toulmin Schema (Toulmin, S.E., 2003) logical argumentation structures. This work evolved into the design of Aquanet (Marshall et al., 1991), a tool strongly concerned with the collaborative knowledge structuring tasks and with the match between a simple data model (associating hypertext concepts with frame-based representations) and an appropriate graphical representation, as a powerful facilitator of collaborative process.

The general and universal process of "writing" was addressed in a structured way by SEPIA (*Structured Elicitation and Processing of Ideas for Authoring*) (Streitz et al., 1989, 1993). Based on a set of writing theories, and also with a focus on argumentative texts, SEPIA incorporates the Toulmin Schema in a rich interactive environment and organizes the authoring tool in different "activity spaces" – *content space*, *planning space*, *rhetorical space* and *argumentation space*. These design options showed how a hypermedia tool could embed support for both the different tasks and meta-tasks of an authoring process (collaborative writing in this case) and the different requirements for logically and semantically structured content.

Dolphin (Haake et al., 1994; Streitz et al., 1994; Mark et al., 1996), developed by the same group at GMD, explored different degrees of flexibility in the interfaces and data models to assure better effectiveness in the support for the collaborative design processes. Interaction styles and seamless transitions between reasoning and activity spaces are contributions to dissolve the cognitive breakdowns introduced by computer-based tools and, therefore, to improve the use of these tools as intellectual augmentation devices.

3.7 THE MEDIA EVOLUTION

The multimedia nature of the information systems and services has been present since the early days of hypertext systems design. Images, graphics and audio/speech elements have been considered in pioneering systems such as NLS/Augment. However, the defining evolution step took place with the adaptation of the fundamental data models, as well as of the representation and interaction techniques, to dynamic media such as audio and video where the temporal dimension is essential.

The reflection on, and design over, the time dimension (Buchanan, M.C. and Zellweger, P.T., 1993; Guimarães et al., 1992) and its smooth integration in hypermedia systems, laid out the ground for the design and development of the Amsterdam Hypermedia Model, already mentioned above, and a number of information structuring concepts and technologies such as HyTime or SMIL, which we describe below.

In any case, the strong integration of dynamic media in hypermedia publishing systems has not been as effective as other dimensions of information integration. Video-intensive services like

YouTube (Time Magazine Person/Invention of the Year 2006), are taking the first steps in the extension of video material with hypertextual structure (see *YouTube*'s Video Annotations presented in 2008). The embedding of videos (both real video and animated sequences) in Flash players, which in turn have been integrated with current web browsers, has been the most significant development contributing to the spreading of dynamic media in hypermedia spaces.

The short review we present here is intended to provide some insights on relevant issues but is by no means a thorough review of multimedia authoring systems, which falls out of the scope of this lecture.

Athena Muse (Hodges et al., 1989) was one of the first comprehensive proposals to approach the construction of multimedia applications in a structured and generic way, to link the construction principles with hypermedia concepts and real information structures and to position multimedia (dynamic media) intensive systems in the context of the previous hypermedia system designs. The package concept of Athena Muse integrated video, text and graphics taking into account the desired synchronization constraints. Then, packages could be connected or linked together into directed graph structures, becoming, therefore, structured nodes of a hypermedia information network in the context of a coherent data model.

Hyperspeech (Arons, B., 1991) is a hypermedia speech-based information space where users can navigate through information elements of recorded speech using speech recognition and getting feedback and control indications through synthesized speech. The system clearly illustrates the possibility of generalization of the hypermedia concepts and design principles to different media.

HyperCafe (Sawhney et al., 1996) is a very relevant contribution to the broadening and intensification of the hypertext concept towards the video space. The idea of "hypervideo" is sharply presented and the comprehensive approach to linking in video enriched spaces (temporal linking, spatial linking, spatio-temporal links and opportunities) provides the fundamental design tools for building computationally effective but also aesthetically sound hypervideo environments.

Other works (Lewis et al., 1996; Hirata et al., 1996; Blackburn, S. and DeRoure, D., 1998; Chambel, T. and Guimarães, N., 2002; Romero, L. and Correia, N., 2003) discuss principles and techniques to support the awareness of a navigational context in video- and other media- based hypermedia systems, mapping well established concepts and techniques from hypertext navigation aids and rhetoric onto the space of dynamic media.

CHAPTER 4

Information and Structured Documents

The design of information as structured documents has been a long and continuous challenge for those who write, publish and interpret documents in their most diverse formats. The identification of multiple-level components (e.g., chapters, sections, subsections, annotations) and relationships between them constitutes the core of a **logical structure** that aims at the improvement of the document clarity and expressiveness, as well as its maintainability, reuse and evolution.

Indexing, through tables of contents or tables of figures as a means of direct access to content, is also often a direct consequence of structure as it is the basis of layout and formatting. In fact, even in a traditional publishing process, the different components were marked-up by an editor to be printed in some way or another. That markup is regularly based on the logical structure but defines the **presentation structure** of the document. Since the early days of digital information storage and management, designers and developers tried to separate the two dimensions, logical structure and presentation, gaining in efficiency, effectiveness and reuse. The search for languages dedicated to each one of these facets and for default rules of mapping between them has also been explored, even before the appearance and dissemination of digital documents.

With the advent of electronic publishing, the crucial issues related with document structure gained further significance (see, for example, the extensive annotated bibliography report by (Furuta, R., 1992)). Document structure is one of the pillars of document preparation tools, such as editors, text processors or text formatters, information retrieval systems or in general information systems.

The document preparation and management tools usually build on a formal or semi-formal structure of the documents they handle to offer automated features, like index generation or navigation support, coherence (e.g., between logical and presentation aspects) and even search and query functionality. Examples of these are the new levels of structure that provide (meta-) meta-information on content and form (Coombs et al., 1987). The digital dimension and the consequent easiness of dissemination is also based on structure for compatibility between different tools and systems and, therefore, frequently leads to the standardization of the document structure.

From its early origins, hypermedia systems were closely associated with structured documents. The notions of multi-level data elements, hierarchical components, cross-component referencing, and separation of the information logical structure from the information presentation were all discussed previously. Inevitably, the evolution of those systems and structured document models and tools reveals a countless number of intersections even though the corresponding communities were, and still are, somehow divided. A corollary of that undisputed symbiosis is of course the World Wide

Web, an immense hypermedia system that adopted the structured document model as a design principle and is currently the platform for most of the advances in document structuring models and technologies.

4.1   THE ORIGINS

The historical background of structured documents, parallel to the emergence of hypertext and hypermedia systems, can be traced back through several distinct paths (André et al., 1989; Furuta, R., 1992; Goldfarb, C., 1996; DITA, 2009). Undoubtedly, though, some milestones indelibly paint all of them. The presentation of William Tunnicliffe on the separation of information content of documents from their format at the Canadian Government Printing Office in September 1967 was certainly one of those. That presentation generated the early concerns for the need of "*markup languages*" or, as initially designated, "generic coding," as a way to introduce structure upon content (Reid, B.K., 1980; Goldfarb, C.F., 1981). On the same decade, Stanley Rice, a New York book designer, proposed a set of parameterized "*editorial structure*" tags.

In the late seventies, the Scribe system (Reid, B.K., 1980) clarified the separation between logic and presentation and introduced styles separated from the document markup structure. It definitely influenced current languages such as HTML+CSS (see below) or LaTeX (Lamport, L., 1994), the later interestingly criticized by Coombs (Coombs et al., 1987) and owing of course to Knuth's TeX (Knuth, D.E., 1978).

Finally, and not necessarily chronologically (the first publications go back to the beginning of the seventies), we should mention GML (Generalized Markup Language) by Charles Goldfarb, Edward Mosher, and Raymond Lorie (Goldfarb, C.F., 1981). They proposed a generalized markup language, understood by a program or a human interpreter, which included the separation of logic and presentation of documents as well. GML was widely used in IBM by that time and is considered the precursor of SGML, the first full standard markup system for structured documents (Goldfarb, C., 1990).

4.2   REFERENCE STANDARDS

Contrary to the profusion of systems that evolved from the early hypertext systems, most of the consolidated work around markup languages and structured documents progressed around the original proposal of SGML. This does not mean that other attempts, like ODA (ISO, 1989a) or specific formatting tools and languages did not emerge from the original approaches, but that most of those that kept a close relation with the hypermedia concepts found in the SGML model the necessary constructs to achieve their objectives.

SGML (Goldfarb, C., 1990), standing for Standard Generalized Markup Language, is an ISO standard (ISO, 1986) that provides a notation for the definition of markup languages. It is thus a meta-language. The grammar of a specific markup language or dialect is defined as a Document Type Definition (DTD). A grammar is essentially composed of a set of object definitions (a lexical set) and a set of valid relations between those objects (a set of syntactic rules). These are then used to validate any instantiation of the dialect, i.e., the documents structured according to the grammar defined in the DTD. Being a very powerful, flexible and, therefore, complex language, SGML supports amongst others, the concepts for logical structuring, but also the constructs for link processing and document validation. Unlike others (e.g., ODA), SGML does not propose any support for the presentation of the document or the interaction styles. **DSSSL** (ISO, 1989b) was designed for that purpose and is composed by a style and a transformation sublanguage. With both languages, it is possible to define the rules that transform the logical structure, specified by an SGML dialect, into a formatted document using a specific formatting language (e.g., in PostScript).

HTML (W3C, 1999) is probably the most known dialect conforming to SGML. Tim Berners-Lee introduced it as the lingua franca of the World Wide Web and immensely reduced the complexity of SGML. It provides simple mechanisms for document structuring (e.g., <div>, <h1>, <h2>…<table>, <img>), simple unidirectional links (href="url") between components of the same or different documents, basic anchoring (<a>, strongly befuddled with linking), data collection elements (<input>), but also some formatting and styling (<b>, <i>). Ideally, the format instantiation and the behavior of any HTML document is standard and should be implemented in the same form by all HTML processors, embedded in the different Web browsers.

The evolution of HTML until HTML 4.0 was craved by the introduction of new markup tags and features that sometimes blurred the separation of the documents' logical structure and presentation directives.

CSS (W3C, 2009a), the Cascade Style Sheet Language introduced by W3C, aimed at clarifying that separation, much in the sense of the style sublanguage of DSSSL. CSS is a declarative language that enables the association of styling properties (e.g., color, size) to specific components of component types of an HTML document. In its second version, CSS2.0 extends its capabilities into media-specific styles (e.g., audio, video, specific devices), thinner layout control, etc.

HyTime (ISO, 1997), another ISO standard, is a SGML application. Its contributions are twofold: (a) to provide richer linking concepts, and (b) to introduce the temporal dimension into documents. On the former, HyTime provides the mechanism to specify complex, bidirectional, typed, and multi-terminated links. The anchoring notion is separated from the link and links become first order components. Regarding the temporal dimension, HyTime allows the specification of temporal events (e.g., *begin*, *end*) in the documents' components. Overall, HyTime provides an integrated perspective of the temporal, spatial and hypermedia dimensions of a document (Roisin, C., 1998) and is a solid contribution to the support of the hypermedia nature in systems based on the structured document approach.

XML (W3C, 2006) is a simplification of SGML that maintains its meta-language nature. In fact, it can be considered an operational version of SGML that has into account the Web requirements. It restricts the power and flexibility of SGML, by specifying, for instance, a particular form for tags, but it provides interesting mechanisms, like namespaces for modularity. It also allows the existence of documents without a DTD as long as they conform to basic XML rules, along with documents validated trough a DTD grammar. XML is being adopted as a *de facto standard* meta-language for the Web but also for other purposes (e.g., information exchange and data storage/retrieval).

As SGML, also XML, has its presentation or formatting language companion: XSL (W3C, 2009b). **XSL** (eXtensible Stylesheet Language) inherits its concepts from DSSSL adopting the XML syntax. It is also composed by a style sublanguage, XSL-FO, and a transformation one, XSLT.

A new version of HTML, XHTML was proposed as an XML valid dialect. XHTML is a revision of the HTML functionality, now fully compliant with the XML rules. One of the effects of this normalization is the stronger adaptation and readability of the HTML code to any presentation environment (multiple devices for example) or any XML-based tools. XHTML is, however, closely related and compatible with HTML 4, the current standard publishing language of the Web. All the developments are up to date in the World Wide Web Consortium information sites.

Once XML became established, dialects for specific domains started to emerge, exploiting the data standardization and interchange capacities. Some of them, like MathML[1], are now W3C recommendations, but the proposals in heterogeneous domains are hard to count. Interesting examples are Systems Biology Markup Language, SMBL, Chemical Markup Language, CML, Geography Markup Language, GML, or Music Markup Language, MusicXML or MML.

This growth of opportunities is based on the flexibility of the XML DTD, which can be designed and hosted anywhere in the network, on the capacity of the hypermedia viewers i.e., the current we browsers to read the XML data together with the required DTD's) and on the integration of viewers for the specific type of information (molecular structures in CML, maps in GML, music scores in MML). The XML generators for these information types still tend to be specialized tools, or tools that have been extended to generate the proper XML dialect (Fig. 4.1 (a), (b), and (c)).

Figure 4.1: (a) The first measure of the "These Foolish Things"[2] score.

XLink, standing for XML Linking Language (W3C, 2001), has a direct correspondence with the link component of HyTime, providing similar functionality, again through a XML-like syntax, and a strong influence from the data models mentioned above.

In its broad objectives, XML Linking attempts to set up an environment where conventional unidirectional links are supported, but more complex linking concepts and mechanisms can be designed. As stated in the XLink W3C recommendation, XLink allows to establish associations

---

[1] www.w3.org/Math.
[2] Credits to Link, Marvel and Strachey.

```xml
<?xml version="1.0" encoding="UTF-8"?>
<!DOCTYPE score-partwise PUBLIC "-//Recordare//DTD MusicXML 2.0 Partwise//EN"
                               "http://www.musicxml.org/dtds/partwise.dtd">
<score-partwise version="2.0">
  <movement-title>these foolish things</movement-title>
  <identification>
    <creator type="composer">Link, Marvel and Strachey</creator>
    <encoding>
      <software>Finale NotePad 2009 for Windows</software>
      <software>Dolet Light for Finale NotePad 2009</software>
      ...
    </encoding>
  </identification>
  ...
<part-list>
    <score-part id="P1">
      <part-name>Bb Clarinet</part-name>
      <score-instrument id="P1-I3">
        <instrument-name>Instrument3</instrument-name>
      </score-instrument>
      <midi-instrument id="P1-I3">
        <midi-channel>1</midi-channel>
        <midi-program>67</midi-program>
        <volume>80</volume>|
        <pan>0</pan>
      </midi-instrument>
    </score-part>
  </part-list>
  <!--=========================================================-->
  <part id="P1">
    <measure number="1" width="341">
      <print>
        <system-layout>
```

Figure 4.1: (b) Generated MusicXML, or MML (part I).

between more than two resources (multi-point links), associate metadata with links (typed links), and refer to links that are not in the same location as the linked content (links as first order objects). Needless to say, the design of XLink has been strongly influenced by the standards and experience with the systems that we revisited in the previous chapter.

SMIL (Bulterman, D., 2001; W3C, 2008) explicitly addresses the temporal dimension of structured hypermedia documents. In this case, however, the temporal concepts of HyTime are extended, and SMIL documents allow the specification of time-based structural composition assuming the existence of multiple, relative timelines for the document.

```
      </score-part>
   </part-list>
   <!--================================
   <part id="P1">
     <measure number="1" width="341">
       <print>
         <system-layout>
         ...
         </system-layout>
       </print>
       <attributes>
         <divisions>12</divisions>
         <key>
           <fifths>1</fifths>
           <mode>minor</mode>
         </key>
         <time symbol="common">
           <beats>4</beats>
           <beat-type>4</beat-type>
         </time>
         <clef>
           <sign>G</sign>
           <line>2</line>
         </clef>
         <transpose>
           <diatonic>-1</diatonic>
           <chromatic>-2</chromatic>
         </transpose>
       </attributes>
       <sound tempo="100"/>
       <note default-x="105">
         <rest/>
         <duration>9</duration>
         <voice>1</voice>
         <type>eighth</type>
         <dot/>
       </note>
       <note default-x="141">
         <pitch>
           <step>G</step>
           <octave>4</octave>
         </pitch>
         <duration>3</duration>
         <voice>1</voice>
         <type>16th</type>
         <stem default-y="1">up</stem>
       </note>
```

Figure 4.1: (c) Generated MusicXML, or MML (part II).

CHAPTER 5

Web-Based Environments

For the sake of the evolutionary analysis we are carrying out here, we will consider the class of systems based on HTML (from the original HTML to subsequent versions), the HTTP protocol and the set of known browsers, from *Mosaic* as the ground-breaking one (not forgetting *Lynx*, the alphanumeric browser for simple terminals), to *Netscape*, then Microsoft *Explorer* and *Firefox*, or Apple's *Safari* or Google's *Chrome*. All these browsers, mainly due to the compliance and compatibility needs, have converged to a common data model and presentation styles. Apart from some *look* & *feel* differences, the linking model, the anchor specification solutions, the generic presentation options (even the "*tab*" model became a de facto standard in window organization), and the support for active elements (like ActiveX controls, Java or Javascript components, Adobe Flash programs) have become pervasive with some (annoying but minor) variations that do not change the fundamental models, interaction styles and functionalities. In this context, we will use the designation "*Web 1.0*" (Berners-Lee et al., 1994; Berners-Lee, T., 2005; Hendler et al., 2008) (taking into account the new wording Web 2.0 that is described below), and we will not go into further details, apart from those already outlined in the previous chapter.

The introduction of the term "*Web 2.0*" is associated with the O'Reilly publishing company, probably the most faithful publisher to the evolution of the Internet, computing systems and related services. The term "Web 2.0" became a tag for a number of systems, existing and promised. The time and effort spent all over the academic and industrial world in the interpretation of this label has surely been immense in the recent years. Rather than getting involved in that debate, we will refer to the presentation of the involved participants (url: `http://oreilly.com/web2/archive/what-is-web-20.html`).

In the context of this lecture, it is however relevant, and wise, to identify the main information and interaction functionalities and solutions that have become common in the so called Web 2.0 applications as they relate closely with some of the primitive functionalities of hypertext and hypermedia systems.

The *collaborative dimension* at the scale of the Web is one of the defining characteristics. This collaboration occurs in the explicit context of multiuser applications, designed for group activity, meant to share personal information, share conversations, and produce information collectively. These design principles are a significant difference from the implicit collaboration through information sharing that was provided by the former web environments. Collaborative work has extended its scope to such a large scale that the notion of the social web has emerged almost naturally and has become a key research and development direction (see below). From the design and technological perspective, this evolution has taken a step further in systems like Second Life, integrating collaboration and 3D environments[1].

The technical and conceptual *blurring between author and reader roles* is another important characteristic of many current web based systems. Following the above lead, writing information became, in may applications, a collaborative writing process, and the *Wikipedia (*www.wikipedia.org*)* style, a collectively built and reviewed encyclopedia, meant a radical shift from the former electronic or digital Encyclopedia type of systems. The same effect can be identified in the explosion of the blogging movement where the hidden author in each one of the web users was liberated from the obligation of becoming a Web Designer, HTML programmer or WWW administrator.

While the primitive models and concepts remain at the core of the Web 2.0 technology, additional functionality has been defined that changes qualitatively the original concepts. The *RSS* (Really Simple Syndication) model of subscription is a significant evolution of the reference link concept and should be considered as a new type of link, or at least a *new type of association*, into the direction of bidirectional and active connections.

The class of Web 2.0 systems enhanced the architectural designs with a strong focus on *peer-to-peer (P2P)* communication, as opposed to the centralized client-server architectures of the primitive hypermedia systems or even the complete mutual independence of web servers. Other technological improvements have been pushed, such as more and more *flexible programming models* (XML over HTTP, Ajax as "JavaScript and XML") and a strong emphasis on the *enhancement of the user experience*, which is also blurring the idea of the web as a document publishing and navigation space but turning it into a space of services and activities.

Globally, the web servers, the web clients, and the information systems behind all them became a platform where services can be designed, provided, and shared by active and participative communities of users. This technological landscape, now available almost universally, has allowed for new designs of systems that were previously conceived as standalone, independent services.

This new space for design opportunities has been adopted and exploited by large-scale information systems and services like the digital libraries group of systems. An interesting example, among many others that are possible, is provided by **Europeana**[2], a large European project that aims at building an open digital library, integrating digital resources, or objects from multiple and heterogeneous sources of multiple and heterogeneous types (see Fig. 5.1 below).

Europeana is targeted at a multiplicity of users wishing to access multimedia resources provided by world-wide providers. Functionally, as their designers state, "the central principle for building Europeana is that a network of semantic resources will be used as the primary level of user interaction. The user will primarily interact with the semantic network to explore the Europeana surrogate space (surrogates being representatives of original objects and their digital representations that remain located at the content provider sites). Europeana can thus be thought of as a network of inter-

---

[1]www.secondlife.com.
[2]www.europeana.eu.

Figure 5.1: Europeana, one example of contemporary technical design for a digital library and related information services.

operating contextualized object surrogates enabling semantics based object discovery and use. This network is an integral part of the overall information architecture of the WWW.

The key issues for a large information service like Europeana are metadata management (access, definition, integration, mapping), object management (identification, access, reuse and exchange), and query and interrogation languages. To address these issues, common protocols and access mechanisms have to be defined and adopted at all levels, like the OAI (Open Archive Initiatives) – with its multiple specifications (PMH – Protocol for Metadata Harvesting[3], ORE – Object Reuse and Exchange[4]), or SRU (Search/Retrieval via URL, this one maintained by the Library of Congress[5]).

The integration and aggregation of massive amounts of digital objects on the common web-based platform will provide a host of new information services. In many of the current designs, however, we should note that the navigational nature of hypertext systems, and, moreover, its serendipity characteristics, are still not clearly understood and fully developed.

---

[3]http://www.openarchives.org/OAI/openarchivesprotocol.html.
[4]http://www.openarchives.org/ore/1.0/toc.html.
[5]http://www.loc.gov/standards/sru/cql-bibliographic-searching.html.

CHAPTER 6

Some Research Trends

The evolution of the research directions in hypermedia information systems has consolidated the basic concerns on the topics that we described above, namely on **systems architecture**, **paradigms and semantics of information linking** and the conceptual **rhetorical** aspects of non-linear writing. These are, and will most probably continue to be, intrinsic topics of our class of systems.

On the other hand, at least two very significant research domains should be highlighted here, as a recognition of current research contributions and as windows to future developments and expected functionality of hypermedia information systems and services. The first domain encompasses the work on "*adaptive hypermedia systems.*" The second domain can be broadly defined as "*social linking.*"

6.1   ADAPTIVE HYPERMEDIA

Since the early concept formation and along the successive designs, hypermedia systems have been concerned with the creation and storage of interlinked information, to its presentation and inter-action, and to generic and global problems like navigation. Broadly speaking, there has been, for a long time, a lack of focus on the specificities of the human users and their contexts while reading and authoring hypermedia information.

The research on Adaptive Hypermedia systems (AH) has emerged in the late 90's and con-solidated in recent years as a significant trend in the evolution of hypermedia systems. Adapta-tion has multiple dimensions, from adaptation of content selection, adaptation of navigation and search support, and adaptation of presentation solutions (De Bra et al., 1999; Kobsa et al., 2001; Brusilowski et al., 2002; De Bra et al., 2002). Concepts that are included in our primitive traits, like *typed links* for example, or more general evolutions like the *semantic web* proposals, are central to the designs and solutions being sought to make hypermedia systems better adapted to their user-specific and contextualized use.

6.2   SOCIAL LINKING

The growth of the Web and its universal impact in multiple dimensions has influenced the orientation and focus of research topics in hypermedia information systems and services. One of the most relevant developments in recent years has been the impact of the so-called Web2.0 applications and tools that reinvented some of the main traits of those hypermedia services, as we mentioned and defined above. The cooperative trait that was inherent to many of the influential systems was expanded and qualitatively transformed by the scale of the web growth and cooperation between groups evolved towards social interaction and social construction of information systems and services. The links and associations between people, for example in `www.{hi5|Facebook|twitter}.com`, have created a new network to be associated, matched, used in conjunction, with the immense network of information and services.

Therefore, it does not come as a surprise (stated *a posteriori* as most predictions) that a growing focus of hypermedia research work falls now under the label *social linking*.

A clear trend is the extrapolation of functionality of hypermedia systems as collaborative and group cognition tools to the broader environment of social cognition, encompassing communities of a larger scale. This social dimension, already approached in previous works (Mark et al., 1996) on hypermedia systems usage, became orders of magnitude larger with the advent of the social web (Wang, W. and Rubart, J., 2006; Al-Khalifa, H.S. and Davis H.C., 2007; Adamic, L.A., 2008).

The integration of larger networked communities with hypermedia information systems and services has also qualitative implications in specific processes related with information access and or hypertextual navigation. This impact is analyzed and discussed, for example, in the case of navigation in (video-based) web lectures (Mertens et al., 2006) or in the case of building social support for information space understanding (Farzan et al., 2007).

A more challenging dimension of the extension of hypermedia systems into a larger community and/or information space is the progressive convergence between information systems and services with the ubiquitous computing and ambient intelligence paradigms. The progressive interaction and integration between physical spaces, augmented with interactive artifacts, and virtual spaces, built and grown in digital networked environments, will have a definite impact on the processes of interaction with information and with hypermedia information services. These last concepts are having a growing impact on the design of computing systems, and the hypermedia information structures will play an important role in the new contexts (Grønbæk, K., 2006; Hansen, F.A. and Grønbæk, K., 2008).

CHAPTER 7

A Framework of Traits

Having reviewed and highlighted some of the relevant characteristics of the above systems and technologies, we are now able to proceed to the definition of a traits framework. The next step is the comprehensive association between systems and traits, which will further lead to a phylogenetic analysis of these hypermedia technology exemplars.

The analysis framework we propose is presented below. Each one of the leaves of this tree is a particular trait that we will redefine here for the sake of clarity and to condensate the understanding of this (phenotypical) element. From then on, we will use the classification presented here.

An important remark must be introduced here. The traits below aim at discriminating recognizable and distinct feature of the reviewed systems. As one might expect, these traits are not orthogonal, nor mutually exclusive, meaning that when we identify one of them in a given system; this should not mean that the system does not show any other trait to some extent. Let us take for example the traits "Simple Links" versus "Bi-directional" versus "Typed Links." Any system supporting bi-directional links generally supports simple links as we should expect, and the same argument holds for the systems that, by supporting typed links also naturally support simple links.

The fact is that many particular systems have proposed a given trait and have emphasized it as a fundamental contribution to demonstrate specific behavior or structure of the hypermedia system. This is the rationale for this classification. As an anticipated overview, we present the list of characteristics below.

A. Link and Association Typology

- A.1 Simple Links or Reference Links

- A.2 Replacements, Expansions and Anchors

- A.3 Bi-Directional Links

- A.4 Typed Links

- A.5 Dynamic (Scripted) Links

- A.6 Links as First Order Objects

- A.7 Multi-Point Links

B. Interaction Styles and Support

- B.1 Card Presentation Style

- B.2 Scrollable Pages/Nodes

A. LINK AND ASSOCIATION TYPOLOGY

A.1 SIMPLE LINKS OR REFERENCE LINKS

This type of link design is the basic and simplest solution proposed by early systems. The presentation solutions varied from special symbols to simple graphics. In general, simple or reference links are point-to-node links where the actual node definition depends on the data/presentation model. Classical "*buttons*" can be considered as examples of this type of basic link mechanisms.

A.2 ANCHORS, REPLACEMENTS AND EXPANSIONS

Linking designs have evolved into multiple alternatives beyond point-to-node or point-to-point association. The first element of evolution in the link concept definition is the *Anchor* concept; which is the specification of the data segments that are the origin and/or destination of links. A sufficiently powerful and generic specification of this concept had impact in the capability to link between nodes of heterogeneous media types.

The replacement or expansion of a segment of data (conceptually equivalent to a local anchor), like a line text, for an expanded set of data, like a new set of paragraphs, is a mechanism that induces data segmentation while maintaining an implicit structured model, essentially hierarchical.

A.3 BI-DIRECTIONAL LINKS

The definition of bidirectional links assumes that for every link between a two elements of an hypermedia information system, there is, automatically and implicitly, a symmetric link, associating destination and origin, or, as it is also frequently defined, a *back link*. *Back links* are important for navigation support, but are also critical for maintaining the consistency of the hypermedia graph or network. Without back links, or a replacement mechanism, the deletion of a node naturally leads to the appearance of "dangling links" (links with no destination) in the nodes that are "pointing" to that first deleted node. On the other hand, the maintenance of the consistency in the hypermedia network raises scalability questions and can only be assured by systems with dedicated storage server, or hyperbase, even if they adopt a distributed or federated model of association.

A.4 TYPED LINKS

The association of attributes to links has been proposed in early systems and data models. The explicit association of types, or a type system, to links, allows the hypermedia network to develop the representational capacity of a semantic network, together with the power of interactive navigation. Typed links, even if possible and available in several systems, have been more intensively used in contexts that use hypermedia systems as knowledge representation environments or as spaces for structured cooperation, i.e., implementing social protocols based on creation and sharing of semantically tagged information structures.

A.5 DYNAMIC AND SCRIPTED LINKS

Dynamic, or scripted, links are links with no predefined destination. The destination of this type of links is computed at selection time, based on the execution of a script in a particular activation context. In the extreme solution, small programs are associated to objects in a node implement links. In a less radical form, links are specified as such, with anchor specifications and default destinations, but can also have associated programs or trigger computational processes.

A.6 LINKS AS FIRST ORDER OBJECTS

The basic, or atomic, elements of a hypermedia network are nodes and links, organized according to some structuring concepts defined by a particular data model. Links are considered to be first class objects if they are addressable independently of other objects, for example, independently from the node of origin. Links as first class objects are typically stored in a link database, have a unique identifier, and include references/addresses and anchor definition data for origin and destination. Addressable links allow for links to links, increasing the flexibility of the information network.

A.7 MULTI-POINT LINKS

Multi-point links associate an origin point or anchor with multiple destinations. The set of destinations can be specified statically or dynamically, and the selection of the destination can be performed computationally or by the user through some user interface mechanism, as for example, a simple menu associated with the origin anchor.

B. INTERACTION STYLES AND SUPPORT

B.1 CARD PRESENTATION STYLE

Many early systems have adopted the card metaphor as the basic information structuring and presentation/interaction unit, following faithfully the Memex concepts and projections. This choice has strong implications in the way information should be segmented in relatively small information units with high granularity and in the rhetorical needs of the textual content. In addition, a network of cards induces a particular interaction and navigation style, characterized by frequent selections of multiple cards.

B.2 SCROLLABLE PAGES/NODES

Contrasting with the card metaphor, the information network can be structured in elements/nodes with larger granularity presented as scrollable pages. This solution is typically associated with a document-based paradigm, most often structured documents, and imposes weaker constraints in the information design, for example in what concerns the rhetorical needs of a hypertextual document.

B.3 OVERLAPPING WINDOWS

The presentation styles of hypermedia information systems have followed the alternatives adopted by the primordial windowing systems. Some systems adopted the overlapping windows option, allowing the several nodes to be presented simultaneously in a free screen positioning mode.

B.4 FRAME PRESENTATION MODEL

As an alternative to the previous presentation style, some hypermedia systems have constrained the presentation of nodes to a reduced number of tiled frames. From early systems to current information browsers, the adoption of frames as the basic screen real estate organization mechanism has become generalized. Frames can be defined in the presentation component of structured document languages or supported by the browsers/viewers with multiple variations; some of them turned into de facto standard functionalities (like the tab concept in most of the current browsers). In any case, this approach aims at enforcing some presentation cohesion in the interaction with hypermedia information systems and services and, therefore, limits the possible disorientation effects of multiple overlapping windows.

B.5 DIAGRAMMATIC REPRESENTATIONS

The size and density of the network of small information units suggested the design of visual and diagrammatic representations used as navigation aids and understanding devices. From simple graph drawing techniques to highly complex representations of the hypermedia network, as for example fish-eye views, diagrammatic representations or visual maps, these are an attempt to facilitate a global understanding of the information structure, to provide additional orientation functionality and, in less frequent cases, to support high-level authoring of the information structure.

B.6 SCRIPTING LANGUAGES

Many hypermedia information structures and services have frequently been supported by interpreted scripting languages, designed and implemented to support some level of programmable dynamic behavior associated with the presentation and navigation, and to integrate some computational capacity. Some early systems have definitely established this component as a necessary functionality, and current systems incorporate it almost universally. These languages are to be considered separately from the document description languages that have become generalized.

B.7 SEARCH AND QUERY

Search and query as a paradigm for information access was not a primary concern of hypermedia systems. In some references, "search and query" is actually considered as heterodoxy, meaning that it deviates from the original and pure navigational paradigm of hypertext. However, some system designs and discussions have assumed the importance of the early integration of search and query tools. It should be noted, as we mentioned above, that the current level of integration of information systems through generalized linking and crossed reference is the fundamental background support for search engines and its web crawler components.

C. DATA MODELS AND INFORMATION STRUCTURE

C.1 SIMPLE COMPOSITION/AGGREGATION STRUCTURES

The simple network structure defined by the node and link concepts requires a minimal level of structuring capacity provided by some aggregation concepts. The simplest ones define grouping structures, more or less self contained, more or less open to external linking. These simple models are essentially flat, i.e., they do not provide hierarchical, nesting or composition concepts and mechanisms.

C.2 COMPREHENSIVE DATA MODEL (OPEN HYPERMEDIA SYSTEMS)

The evolution of the work on hypermedia data models led, on the first hand, to the formalization and tentative standardization of more complex and comprehensive data models with structured composition mechanisms, rich node/link/anchor concept definitions and logical levels identification as well as with specifications of the appropriate interfaces. These definitions have, in turn, supported the design and implementation of Open Hypermedia Systems, which are based on shared and open data models and on clear logical interfaces, namely between interaction and storage levels.

C.3 STRUCTURED DOCUMENTS AND TAGGED INFORMATION

The internal structure of the information elements integrated in a hypermedia system has been a division criteria for many information systems. The purest ones tended to separate completely the content from structure and linking. Others assumed the tradition of document description languages or markup languages, and considered that the structural information as well as the linking information could be merged with the actual content. As we know now, this has been the generalized solution for large-scale systems where the alternative of storing structural/linking information separate from the content raises scalability and consistency problems that are probably impossible to overcome.

C.4 SIMPLE MULTIMEDIA

Images, graphics and sound have been considered obvious information types for hypermedia nodes and have been supported since the early days. In general, the simple solution of many systems has been to consider these nodes as "blocks of multimedia data," or bulk data, or as the database systems has classified them, BLOB (Binary Large OBjects). These are presented (displayed, played) as a whole with no concern for their internal structure.

C.5 MULTIMEDIA INTEGRATION AND ANCHORING

The integration of multimedia information in hypermedia systems is richer when the internal structure of the media content is considered, and anchors can be defined in specific locations of the media content. Image maps were the first mechanism to support the selective linking from images. As the multimedia information gets more complex, and especially if it includes a temporal/dynamic dimension, the requirements for anchor specification and management become more complex. Anchor definition can be based in syntactic features (like spatial or temporal spans) but also in content-related features (like a particular object or character in a movie or picture).

D. ARCHITECTURE AND SCALE

D.1 SINGLE USER AND SMALL SCALE

Some hypermedia systems have been designed for individual users, or single user interaction, very much as personal productivity tools, electronic books or encyclopedias.

D.2 GROUP AND COOPERATIVE USAGE

Most of the early and reference hypermedia systems targeted groups of users, interacting concurrently with the hypermedia information structure, sharing the content and the structure, and often engaged in cooperative activities. The target scale of these systems is typically dozens to hundreds of users.

D.3 LARGE SCALE AND GENERALIZED USAGE

A smaller number of hypermedia systems have targeted the global and universal information space. The critical dimension of these systems is the scalability of the linking and information structuring models, its consistency constraints, and the navigational support that can be designed for the target unlimited scale.

D.4 DATA STORAGE SERVERS

The typical mid-scale hypermedia system, designed to support information sharing and cooperation between members of mid-sized groups, is supported by a content server that implements the storage and retrieval functionality. Depending on the adoption of a custom or a standard data model and access interfaces, the storage server architecture may be more or less close to the open hypermedia systems concept mentioned above.

D.5 CONCURRENCY CONTROL AND VERSIONING

Shared access and concurrent authoring of hypermedia information systems introduces new dimensions in the typical concurrency control mechanisms of shared information systems, beyond read/write operations on the data records of a standard relational database, for example. Node and link versioning has been considered with different levels of detail in some reference systems. We decided to merge these two aspects together since they seem to define solutions for similar issues in the problem space of distributed cooperative hypermedia systems.

E. DESIGN AND FUNCTIONAL GOALS

E.1 EXPLICIT COLLABORATIVE ENVIRONMENT

While the notion of information and knowledge sharing and implicit collaboration is pervasive across the whole spectrum of hypermedia systems, some systems were designed to support explicit collaboration processes like argumentation or collaborative writing. These systems based the support for collaboration in semantically-loaded information structures, relying on typed nodes and links explicitly and intentionally organized in dedicated interaction spaces.

E.2 SEAMLESS INTEGRATION OF AUTHOR/READER ROLES

The level of separation between reader and author roles is an important design characteristic of many hypermedia systems and environments. Some systems require the use of dedicated authoring tools, different from the general viewers/browsers, a fact that tend to separate intellectual and work roles. Other systems, and their evolutions, tend to minimize heterogeneity between reading and authoring tools and to provide seamless transitions between both, thus closing in on the original principle that every reader is also an author, and stressing the collaborative, now social, dimension of hypermedia systems.

In the analysis that follows, the first dimension is the list of the discriminating traits presented above. The second dimension is the list of systems, which will be called the operational taxonomical units (OTU), or entities. In our reflection framework, this list is composed of the systems presented above.

- NLS/Augment

- Xanadu

- Hypercard

- KMS

- Guide

- NoteCards

- Intermedia

- HyperTies

- Sepia

- Microcosm

- Hyper-G

- Web (1.0)

- Web (2.0)

CHAPTER 8

A Phylogenetic Analysis

The generic goal of a phylogenetic analysis is to derive a tree representing the evolution of a group of entities or operating taxonomical units based on a set of characters. One of the purposes is to estimate evolutionary relationships among living organisms based on, for example, DNA or protein sequences.

The tools used to perform phylogenetic analysis use a number of stabilized methods, all of them sharing a number of assumptions and a common objective. The assumptions are essentially the following:

- The sequences of characters for each taxonomical unit are homologous and aligned (this is most relevant when using strands of generic material),

- The taxonomical units are descendants of a common ancestor,

- The evolution is based on the basic genetic mechanisms of mutation,

- The entities are assumed to form (ideally) a dichotomously branching tree.

All of these assumptions are implicit in the design of a *data matrix* that condensates the multiple sequences and becomes the critical data set for a conclusive and, possibly correct, phylogenetic tree.

The established methods for phylogenetic analysis fall into three main categories: parsimony, minimum distance and maximum likelihood. A thorough and critical description of each one of these methods is out of the scope of this lecture, and out of the scope of our expertise, but the following is in summary: (a) *parsimony* methods, inspired in classification method known as cladistics (a.k.a. phylogenetic systematics) searches for a tree that minimizes character changes, adopting the simplest explanation for evolution (Stevenson, D., Ed., 1998; Page, R.D.M. and Homes, E.C., 1998; Felsenstein, J., 2002), (b) minimum distance methods minimize pairwise distances between organisms, and (c) maximum likelihood methods search for the evolutionary tree (the hypothesis) that better matches the available data (Salemi, M. and Vandamme A.-M., 2003; Hall, B.G., 2007). These methods are currently implemented by a diversity of software tools known and used by biologists. In our exercise[1], we use *two* available tools, PAUP[2] and MrBayes[3]. The decision to use two different tools that use different methods has the unique purpose to produce a wider range of results and minimize tool specificities.

---

[1]We are specially thankful to Octavio Paulo, our colleague from the Animal Biology Department at the Faculty of Sciences of the University of Lisbon, who took the time and curiosity to apply the phylogenetic analysis tools to our unconventional domain.

[2]http://paup.csit.fsu.edu. – PAUP Phylogenetic Analysis Using Parsimony.

[3]http://mrbayes.csit.fsu.edu. Mr Bayes, a freely available program for bayesian estimation of phylogeny.

8.1   AN EVOLUTIONARY ANALYSIS OF HYPERMEDIA SYSTEMS

In our specific context, as mentioned in the introduction, we have the goal of approaching hypermedia information systems and services as related entities in an evolutionary tree, and should, therefore, follow the procedure of a phylogenetic analysis. Given this particular domain of application, we shall, however, express the following remarks and relaxations:

- The basic assumption that all hypermedia systems derive from an ancestor has a cultural and historical background. We believe that the common principles of information linking and association, of navigation and also knowledge creation that were elicited by the *Memex* system can be considered as a solid common ancestor, or a shared reference to this class of systems, and even taken as an alternative to query-based information systems or to rule-based knowledge systems.

- The *data matrix* (see below) that is the set of multiple character sequences is a subjectively constructed data set where each value is the result of a conceptual and functional evaluation, based on existing bibliography and personal experience. Moreover, the set of characters or traits that was defined above is also the result of a particular interpretation of the authors. As a result, the whole data set is a production of a subjective analysis and classification.

- The basic genetic mechanisms of evolution, like *crossover* or *mutation* (Purves et al., 2004), that are also adopted (by analogy) in computer science in the field of evolutionary computing and more specifically in genetic algorithms (Mitchell, M., 1998), do not have an immediate translation into the space of multiple designs. The design of each one of the analyzed systems has been guided by a diversity of the functional requirements, target user populations, envisaged application domains. On the other hand, in a given problem space (determined by a framework of requirements and objectives), systems have adopted alternative designs and solutions adapted to the requirements and have evolved by alternative or enhancement, sometimes by deletion or rejection of a functionality due to some specific feasibility constraint (for example, scalability objectives versus data consistency objectives). In this context, the basic evolutionary mechanisms are, therefore, to be assumed in its broadest meaning.

- Implicit to the comments above is the limitation of the choice of the evolutionary model that the phylogenetic analysis tools provide. We should not state that a design and functional evolution necessarily adopts the model of living systems. For the time being, we can only proceed qualitatively and be aware of this constraint.

THE DATA MATRIX

We now present a sample version of the data matrix that was applied to our phylogenetic analysis software. The rows of the matrix are the revisited hypermedia systems, or operational taxonomical units (OTU),or *taxa*, in the terminology of many software packages. The columns are the traits defined above, individually considered.

The data matrix represented in Fig. 8.1 is a binary matrix where a "1" means that the trait is present, as a concept, a functionality, a design goal, while the "0" means that trait is not present or considered[4].

A possible second version of the data matrix, sometimes used in phylogenetic analysis, collapses a number of traits and defines a scale of (integer) values to classify the strength or complexity of a given (collapsed) trait. This second approach is said to strengthen the robustness of the analysis. This was not our case and a clear explanation for that remains to be found, except for the fact that collapsing some of our traits into complexity levels would mix up characters that are qualitatively diverse and introduce an additional level of ambiguity in this evolutionary analysis.

	Link and association typology							Interaction styles and support							Data models and information structure					Architecture and Scale						Design and Functional Goals	
	A1	A2	A3	A4	A5	A6	A7	B1	B2	B3	B4	B5	B6	B7	C1	C2	C3	C4	C5	D1	D2	D3	D4	D5	D6	E1	E2
NLS/Augment	1	0	1	0	0	1	0	1	0	1	0	1	1	1	1	0	1	1	0	0	1	0	1	1	0	0	0
Xanadu	1	1	0	1	0	1	0	0	1	0	0	1	1	0	0	1	1	1	1	0	0	1	1	1	0	0	0
Hypercard	0	0	0	0	1	0	1	1	0	0	0	1	0	1	0	0	0	0	0	1	0	0	0	0	0	0	0
KMS	1	0	0	0	0	0	0	1	0	0	1	0	1	0	1	0	0	1	0	0	1	0	1	1	0	0	0
Guide	1	1	0	0	0	0	0	0	1	0	1	0	0	1	1	0	0	1	0	1	0	0	0	0	0	0	0
Notecards	0	1	0	1	0	0	0	1	0	1	0	1	0	0	1	0	0	1	0	0	1	0	1	0	0	1	0
Intermedia	0	1	0	1	0	1	0	0	1	1	0	1	0	0	1	0	0	1	1	0	1	0	1	1	0	0	1
Hyperties	0	1	0	0	1	0	0	0	1	0	1	0	1	1	1	0	1	1	1	1	0	0	0	0	0	0	0
Sepia	0	1	1	1	0	1	0	0	1	1	0	0	0	1	0	1	0	1	1	0	1	0	1	1	1	1	1
Microcosm	1	1	1	1	0	1	1	0	1	1	0	0	0	0	0	1	0	1	1	0	1	0	1	1	1	0	1
Hyper-G	1	0	0	0	0	1	1	0	1	0	1	0	1	1	0	1	1	1	1	0	0	1	1	1	0	0	0
Web (1.0)	1	1	0	0	0	0	0	0	1	1	0	0	1	0	1	0	1	1	0	0	0	1	1	0	0	0	0
Web (2.0)	1	1	1	0	0	0	1	0	1	1	1	0	1	1	1	0	1	1	1	0	0	1	1	0	0	1	1

Column legend (A1–E2):
- A1 Simple links / Reference Links
- A2 Replacements/Expansions/Anchors
- A3 Bi-directional links
- A4 Typed links
- A5 Dynamic (scripted) links
- A6 Links as first order objects
- A7 Multi-point links
- B1 Card presentation style
- B2 Scrollable pages/nodes
- B3 Overlapping Windows
- B4 Frame presentation model
- B5 Diagrammatic representations
- B6 Scripting languages
- B7 Search and query
- C1 Simple composition/aggregation structures
- C2 Comprehensive data model (OHS)
- C3 Structured Documents and Tagged Information
- C4 Simple Multimedia (graphics, images, movies)
- C5 Multimedia Anchoring
- D1 Single user and small scale
- D2 Group and cooperative usage
- D3 Large scale and generalized usage
- D4 Data storage servers
- D5 Concurrency control and Versioning
- D6 Versioning
- E1 Explicit Collaboration Environment
- E2 Seamless integration of author/reader roles

Figure 8.1: Data matrix built of general purpose spreadsheet software.

[4]We avoided the expression of missing information for traits, in spite of its support in the analysis software.

The actual input data for both the PAUP and MrBayes analysis software is an ASCII file (NEXUS format (Madison et al., 1997)) with the format presented below. Once loaded by the analysis software, PAUP or MrBayes, multiple internal commands for the execution of the analysis are required. We will refrain ourselves from entering into those details here.

```
#Nexus
Begin data;
 dimensions ntax=13 nchar=27;
 format datatype=standard missing=? gap=-;
  matrix
NLSA 1 0 1 0 0 1 0 1 0 1 0 1 1 1 1 0 1 1 0 0 1 0 1 1 0 0 0
Xana 1 1 0 1 0 1 0 0 1 0 0 1 1 0 0 1 1 1 1 0 0 1 1 1 0 0 0
Hype 0 0 0 0 1 0 1 1 0 0 0 0 1 1 0 0 0 0 0 1 0 0 0 0 0 0 0
KMSs 1 0 0 0 0 0 0 1 0 0 1 0 1 0 1 0 0 1 0 0 1 0 1 1 0 0 0
Guid 1 1 0 0 0 0 0 0 1 0 1 0 0 1 1 0 0 1 0 1 0 0 0 0 0 0 0
Note 1 0 0 1 0 0 0 1 0 1 0 1 0 0 1 0 0 0 0 0 1 0 1 0 0 1 0
Inte 0 1 1 1 0 1 0 0 1 1 0 1 0 0 1 0 0 1 1 0 1 0 1 1 0 0 0
Hypt 0 1 0 0 1 0 0 0 1 0 1 0 1 1 1 0 1 1 1 1 0 0 0 0 0 0 0
Sepi 0 1 1 1 0 1 0 0 1 1 0 0 0 1 0 1 0 1 1 0 1 0 1 1 1 1 1
Micr 1 1 1 1 0 1 1 0 1 1 0 0 0 0 0 1 0 1 1 0 1 0 1 1 1 0 1
HypG 1 0 1 0 0 1 1 0 1 1 0 1 1 1 0 1 1 1 1 0 0 1 1 1 0 0 0
Web1 1 1 0 0 0 0 0 0 1 1 1 0 1 0 1 0 1 1 0 0 0 1 1 0 0 0 0
Web2 1 1 1 0 0 0 1 0 1 0 1 1 1 0 1 1 1 0 1 1 0 0 0 1 1 0 0 1 1
;
end;
```

Figure 8.2:

NOTE: In the data matrix and the following diagrams, the names of the systems were abbreviated, to meet the requirements of some of the software packages (uniform name lengths for the taxonomical units). The operating designations for the different systems:

NLSA - NLS/Augment

Xana - Xanadu

Hype - Hypercard

KMSs - KMS

Guid - Guide

Note - NoteCards

Inte - Intermedia

```
Hypt - HyperTIES

Sepi - SEPIA

Micr - Microcosm

HypG - Hyper-G

Web1 - Web-based Systems 1.0

Web2 - Web-based Systems 2.0
```

8.2   THE PHYLOGENETIC TREES AND DIAGRAMS

The phylogenetic trees resulting from the analysis are presented in the following set of figures in three different formats (*rectangular cladogram, unrooted cladogram* and *phylogram*). Figures 8.3, 8.4, and 8.5 are the result of the PAUP analysis. Figures 8.6, 8.7 and 8.8 are the output of the MrBayes runs[5].

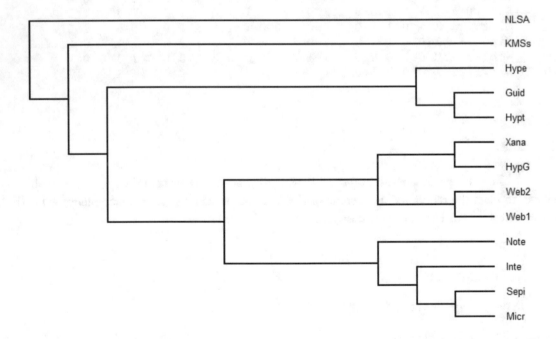

Figure 8.3: Results of the PAUP analysis (*rectangular cladogram*).

[5]The PAUP and MrBayes software generates an ASCII tree representation that can then be viewed and manipulated by the TreeView utility software (http://taxonomy.zoology.gla.ac.uk/rod/treeview.html).

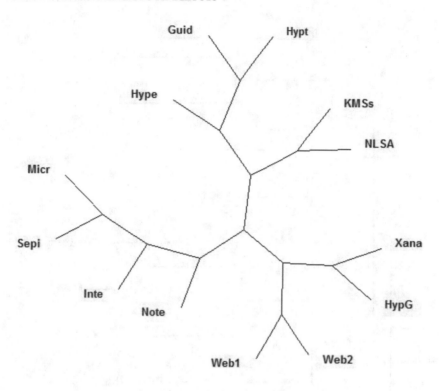

Figure 8.4: Results of the PAUP analysis (*unrooted cladogram*).

PAUP uses a simpler technique called neighbor-joining (NJ) (Saitou, N. and Nei, M., 1987), which, once a distance matrix is built from the data matrix, *taxa* are joined in a pairwise way. MrBayes adopts the Bayesian approach and tries to infer the probability of trees conditioned by the given observations in the data matrix (this is called the posterior probability of the trees). To overcome the impossibility of the analytical calculation of these probabilities, MrBayes uses a Markov Chain Monte Carlo simulation technique. These methods are applied and discussed in their original context of Biology studies in (Paulo et al., 2008), and though this work may seem far from our concerns, we believe it to be an inspiring analogy, and we owe this reference to our fellow biologists.

The analysis software provides a fair amount of additional information. One of the relevant indications is the "clade credibility tree," which gives the probability of each partition or clade in the tree. This is a measure of the robustness of our analysis given, in our context, the initial traits definition, the values chosen for each *system* (taxonomical unit) / *trait* pair, and the default evolution model that was considered. In Fig. 8.9 below, we can see the credibility values for each grouping that

---

[6]The length of the phylogram branches allow the measure of the distances between OUT's, based on the scale indicated in the lower left corner. We do not argue for any particular interpretation of this distance in this analysis context.

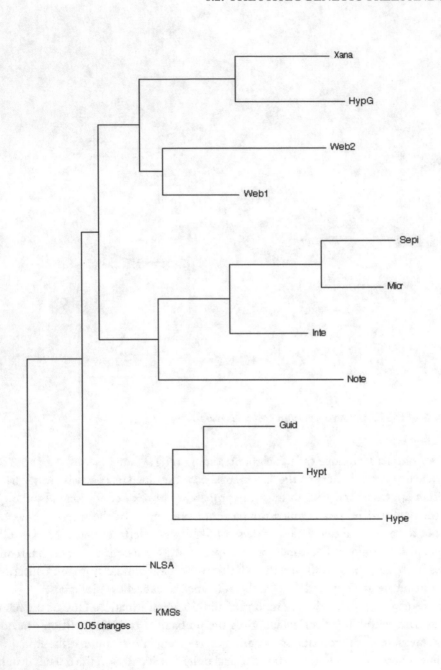

Figure 8.5: Results of the PAUP analysis (*phylogram*)[6].

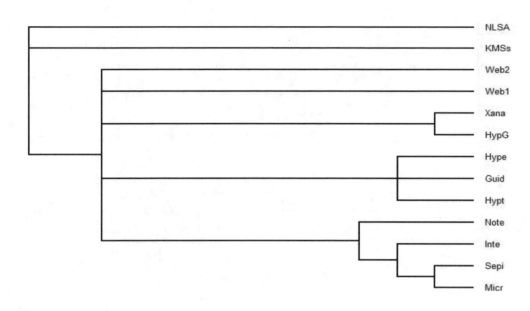

Figure 8.6: Results of MrBayes analysis (*cladogram*).

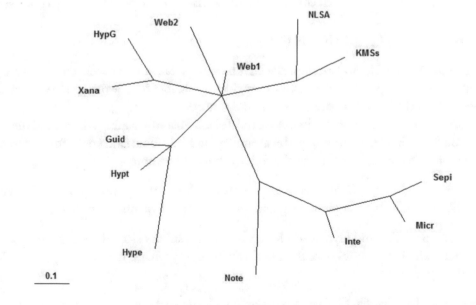

Figure 8.7: Results of MrBayes analysis (*unrooted cladogram*).

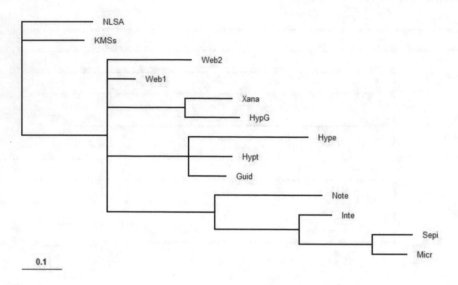

Figure 8.8: Mr Bayes (*phylogram*).

was inferred in the analysis performed with the use of MrBayes software. As we can see, except for the association of SEPIA and Microcosm, the values advise us to be prudent in any conclusion.

8.3   DISCUSSION OF THE ANALYSIS

In spite of all the limitations and assumptions that have to be taken into consideration, and that we mentioned above, we argue that this analysis provides a valuable framework to build a systematic perspective of hypermedia information systems and services.

In both of the experiments, the first, using the distance-based grouping criteria, and the second, adopting a Bayesian inference approach, the groupings and relations match our broad expectations with some interesting variations. In fact, the following should be noted:

- The NLS/Augment and KMS systems are presented separately, most probably because our classification reflects their pioneering and seminal role in hypermedia systems.

- Guide, HyperTIES and HyperCard form a group of systems oriented for single user adoption or small scale. It is also relevant that, in this branch, Hypercard is sufficiently "distant" from the other two systems.

- NoteCards, Intermedia, Sepia and Microscom, cluster together in both analysis. The causes for this clustering are certainly multiple. First, these systems all tend to support groups of users in different application areas, problem spaces and collaborative contexts. Second, these

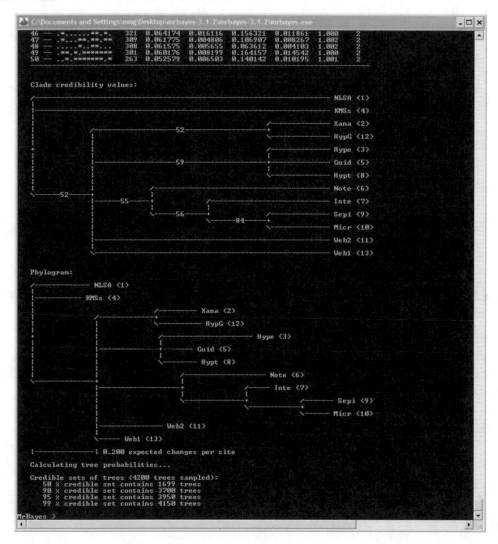

Figure 8.9: (a) Mr Bayes screen after the analysis and cladogram with credibility values.

systems clearly triggered an evolution of several concepts and techniques (like anchoring or typed links). Third, and this is probably the best explanation for the strong credibility of the Microcosm/Sepia clustering, these systems have developed the architectural concepts of hypermedia information services (like the openness of hyperbases, versioning, etc).

The group composed of the large-scale or universal-scale systems also emerges very clearly in the analyses (the second analysis does not provide such elegant results as the first one). Xanadu™ and

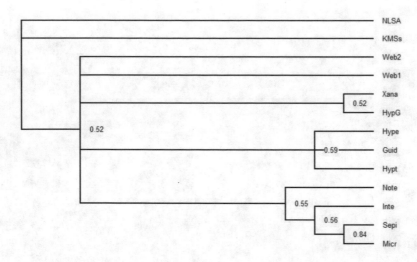

Figure 8.9: (b) Mr Bayes screen after the analysis and cladogram with credibility values.

Hyper-G cluster together most probably for their scalability goals and the higher complexity of some of the information structuring concepts (like transclusion or the bidirectional linking principle). The Web-based systems form a close but distinct group of systems and, as we would expect, the system classified as Web2 is sufficiently distant from Web1.

In the conclusions, we will return to the methodological, and pedagogical, relevance of this approach, as an artifact for system analysis and critique.

CHAPTER 9

Conclusion

Information systems and services show common characteristics, reflecting an historical evolution of the core technology design. Hypertext and hypermedia systems designed, prototyped and implemented in the final part of the last century have triggered an evolution path that led to the creation of a rich set of conceptual devices, a rich number of reference designs, and a solid understanding of the intellectual power of hypermedia-based systems.

General and more or less detailed surveys of hypertext and hypermedia systems have been performed and published by several authors. We believe that there is an intrinsic value in discovering conceptual relations between those systems. To perform that discovery, the construction of a stable framework of traits is an intermediate step. The design of this framework of traits, as with any classification system, is necessarily subjective but includes a number of undisputed dimensions that are shared by the designers and developers of hypermedia systems.

The framework of traits is a classification space where any given system is represented by a particular signature. This signature is a focused classification of a system and supports its further comparative analysis using systematic tools that are used to in many computer science problems.

Once placed in the classification space, we performed a phylogenetic analysis using tools that are typically applied to the study of the evolution of living systems.

The results of the phylogenetic analysis saved us from presenting an ad hoc classification, based on global and subjective views on any of the systems. The traits and the trait signature of each system are naturally open to errors and bias, but we believe that they are anyway independent and allow us to focus on independent and more granular features of each system.

From the results of the analysis, we can confirm a number of clusters: (a) the more personal systems, designed for individual access and navigation (like Hypercard, HyperTies or Guide), showing a common set of traits that can be applied to similar systems in the contemporary platforms; (b) tools for mid-sized groups, for medium scale information systems, and extensively used in collaborative work, which traits should be taken into consideration in future designs; (c) large scale systems, where any analysis of the WWW-based systems leads to an association with the pioneering reference Xanadu™ and with systems that have tried to compensate some of the Web limitations.

It is hard to extrapolate definite orientations for the future systems. This analysis is essentially descriptive, and it would be premature to look for any normative or prescriptive use of this type of analysis. Hypothetically, the requirements definition and conceptual design of any information system, service or tool, can benefit from an early comparative, or even phylogenetic, analysis between its prospective traits signature and previous systems' signatures.

Some of the features of the phylogenetic analysis are debatable when applied to the analysis of the evolution of technological artifacts, as we mentioned previously, in the introduction and in the related chapter. Distance measures, dichotomic trees, and the evolution model implicit in some of the statistical inference techniques have to be evaluated and reviewed in this particular context.

We believe that there is an intrinsic value in this approach and debate, and in this line of questioning. In a coherent analysis framework that produces global results from individual observations, any confirmation or surprise is a valuable contribution to the refinement and systematic correction of our own perspectives and assumptions.

Bibliography

Adamic, L.A. (2008). The social hyperlink, Hypertext '2009 Keynote Address. DOI: 10.1145/1557914.1557916

Akscyn, R.M., McCracken, D.L., and Yoder, E.A. (1988). KMS: A Distributed Hypermedia System for Managing Knowledge in Organizations. Communications of the ACM, 31(7):820–835, July 1988. DOI: 10.1145/48511.48513

Akscyn, R. and McCracken, D. (1993). Plexus: A Hypermedia Architecture for Large-scale Digital Libraries, DL '93. DOI: 10.1145/166025.166028

Akscyn, R.M., McCracken, D.L., and Yoder, E. (1987). KMS: a distributed hypermedia system for managing knowledge in organizations, November 1987, ACM Hypertext '87. DOI: 10.1145/48511.48513

Al-Khalifa, H.S. and Davis, H.C. (2007). Towards better understanding of folksonomic patterns, ACM Hypertext '07. DOI: 10.1145/1286240.1286288

Allison, G.T. and Zelikow, P. (1999). Essence of Decision: Explaining the Cuban Missile Crisis, 2nd ed., Longman, January 1999.

Robinson, A. (1995). The Story of Writing, Thames & Hudson, London, 1995.

André, J., Furuta, R., and Quint, V. (1989). "By Way of an Introduction. Structured Documents: What and Why?". In J. André, R. Furuta and V. Quint (eds.), Structured Documents. Cambridge University Press, 161–181.

Andrews, K., Kappe, F., and Maurer, H. (1995a). Hyper-G and harmony: towards the next generation of networked information technology, May 1995, ACM CHI '95. DOI: 10.1145/223355.223412

Andrews, K., Kappe, F., and Maurer, H. (1995b). The Hyper-G Network Information System, Journal of Universal Computer Science, vol. 1, no. 4 (1995), 206–220. DOI: 10.3217/jucs-001-04-0206

Antoniou, G. and van Harmelen, F. (2008). Semantic Web Primer, 2nd edition (Cooperative Information Systems Series), The MIT Press, 2008.

Arons, B. (1991). Hyperspeech: navigating in speech-only hypermedia, September 1991, ACM Hypertext '91. DOI: 10.1145/122974.122989

Berners-Lee, T. (2005). WWW at 15 years: looking forward, May 2005, WWW'05: Proceedings of the 14th international Conference on World Wide Web. DOI: 10.1145/1060745.1060746

Berners-Lee, T., Cailliau, R., Luotonen, A., Nielsen, H.F., and Secret, A. (1994). The World-Wide Web, August 1994, Communications of the ACM, Volume 37 Issue 8. DOI: 10.1145/179606.179671

Bernstein, M. (1999). Structural patterns and hypertext rhetoric, December 1999, ACM Computing Surveys (CSUR), Volume 31 Issue 4es. DOI: 10.1145/345966.346011

Bernstein, M., Marshall, C.C., and Streitz, N. (1993). Argumentation in action, December 1993, Hypertext '93. DOI: 10.1145/168750.168849

Blackburn, S. and DeRoure, D. (1998). A Tool for Content Based Navigation of Music, ACM Multimedia '98. DOI: 10.1145/290747.290802

Bolchini, D., Garzotto, F., and Paolini, P. (2008). Investigating success factors for hypermedia development tools, June 2008, ACM Hypertext '08. DOI: 10.1145/1379092.1379128

Bolter, J.D. and Grusin, R. (2000). Remediation – Understanding New Media, 2000, MIT Press.

Bolter, J.D. (1991). Writing Space – the Computer, Hypertext, and the History of Writing, Lawrence Erlbaum Associates, 1991.

Boorstin, D.J. (1985). The Discoverers – a History of Man's Search to Know His World and Himself, First Vintage Books Edition, 1985.

Brown, P. (1987). Turning Ideas into Products: The Guide System. ACM Hypertext '87, pp. 199–205.

Brown, P. (1992). UNIX GUIDE: Lessons from ten years' development. ACM ECHT '92, November 1992. DOI: 10.1145/168466.168492

Brown, P. (1994). Adding Networking to Hypertext. Can it be done transparently? ACM ECHT '94. DOI: 10.1145/192757.192769

Brusilowski, P. and Maybury, M.T. (2002). From Adaptive Hypermedia to the Adaptive Web, Communications of the ACM, Vol. 45, nr. 5, May 2002. DOI: 10.1145/506218.506239

Buchanan, M.C. and Zellweger, P.T. (1993). Automatic temporal layout mechanisms, September 1993, ACM MULTIMEDIA '93. DOI: 10.1145/166266.168415

Buford, J.F. (1996). Evaluating HyTime: an examination and implementation experience, March 1996, ACM Hypertext '96. DOI: 10.1145/234828.234839

Bulterman, D. (2001). SMIL 2.0 Part 1: Overview, Concepts, and Structure, IEEE MultiMedia 8(4), Oct-Dez, 2001. DOI: 10.1109/93.959106

Bush, V. (1945). As We May Think., Atlantic Monthly, July 1945, also in Nyce, J.M. and Kahn, P. (eds.), From Memex to Hypertext – Vannevar Bush and the Mind's Machine, Academic Press, 1991.

Campbell, B. and Goodman, J. (1988). HAM: A General Purpose Hypertext Abstract Machine, Communications of the ACM, July 1988. DOI: 10.1145/48511.48515

Catlin, T., Bush, P., and Yankelovich, N. (1989). InterNote: Extending a Hypermedia Framework to Support Annotative Collaboration. ACM Hypertext '89, pp. 365–378, November 1989. DOI: 10.1145/74224.74252

Chambel, T. and Guimarães, N. (2002). Context perception in video-based hypermedia spaces, June 2002, ACM Hypertext '02. DOI: 10.1145/513338.513365

Conklin, J. and Begeman, M.L. (1987). gIBIS: A Hypertext Tool for Team Design and Deliberation, Hypertext '87, November 1987. DOI: 10.1145/317426.317444

Conklin, J. and Begeman, M.L. (1988). gIBIS: a hypertext tool for exploratory policy discussion, October 1988, Transactions on Information Systems (TOIS), Volume 6 Issue 4. DOI: 10.1145/62266.62278

Conklin, J., Selvin, A., Shum, S.B., and Sierhuis, M. (2001). Facilitated hypertext for collective sensemaking: 15 years on from gIBIS, September 2001, ACM Hypertext '01. DOI: 10.1145/504216.504246

Coombs, J.H., Renear, A.H., and DeRose, S.J. (1987). Markup systems and the future of scholarly text processing. Communications of the ACM 30, 11 (Nov. 1987), 933–947. DOI: 10.1145/32206.32209

Davis, H.C. (1999). Hypertext link integrity, December 1999, Computing Surveys (CSUR), Volume 31 Issue 4es. DOI: 10.1145/345966.346026

Davis, H.C., Hall, W., Heath, I., Hill, G., and Wilkins, R. (1992). Towards an Integrated Information Environment with Open Hypermedia Systems. ACM ECHT '92, pp. 181–190. DOI: 10.1145/168466.168522

De Bra, P., Aerts, A., Smits, D., and Stash, N. (2002). AHA! the next generation, June 2002, ACM Hypertext '02. DOI: 10.1145/513338.513347

De Bra, P., Houben, G., and Wu, H. (1999). AHAM: A Dexter-based Reference Model for Adaptive Hypermedia, Proceedings of the ACM Hypertext '99, pp. 147–156, 1999. DOI: 10.1145/294469.294508

Delany, P. and Landow, G.P. (1991). Hypermedia and Literary Studies. The MIT Press, 1991.

DITA (2009). History of DITA.
http://www.ditausers.org/about_us/history_of_dita/#1960.

Dodd, R. (2008). 20 years on: the Dexter Model of Hypertext and its impact on web accessibility, January 2008, SIGACCESS Accessibility and Computing, Issue 90. DOI: 10.1145/1340779.1340780

Durand, D.G. and DeRose, S.J. (1993). FRESS hypertext system (abstract), December 1993, ACM Hypertext '93. DOI: 10.1145/168750.168834

Eco, U. (1998). Serendipities – Language and Lunacy, Phoenix and Columbia University Press, 1998.

Eisenstein, E.L. (1980). The Printing Press as an Agent of Change, Cambridge University Press, Semptember 1980.

Engelbart, D. (1988a). Authorship Provisions in Augment. In Irene Greif, Ed., Computer Supported Collaborative Work: A Book of Readings, pp. 107–127. Morgan Kaufman Publishers, 1988.

Engelbart, D. (1968a). The 1968 Demo,
http://video.google.com, http://www.youtube.com,
http://en.wikipedia.org/wiki/The_Mother_of_All_Demos,
http://www.68anniversary.org.

Engelbart, D. (1988b). Towards High Performance Knowledge Workers. In Greif, I., Ed., Computer Supported Collaborative Work: A Book of Readings, pp. 67–81. Morgan Kaufman, 1988.

Engelbart, D. and English, W. (1968b). A research center for augmenting human intellect, December 1968, AFIPS '68 Proceedings of the 1968 Fall Joint Computer Conference. DOI: 10.1145/1476589.1476645

Engelbart, D. and Nelson, T. (1995). "Toward Augmenting the Human Intellect and Boosting our Collective IQ" and "The Heart of the Connection: Hypermedia Unified by Transclusion," Communications of the ACM - August 1995. DOI: 10.1145/208344.208352

Engelbart, D.C. (1962). AUGMENTING HUMAN INTELLECT: A Conceptual Framework, Stanford Research Institute, SRI Project No. 3578, October 1962.
http://sloan.stanford.edu/mousesite/EngelbartPapers/
B5_F18_ConceptFrameworkInd.html.

Farzan, R., Coyle, M., Freyne, J., Brusilovsky, P., and Smyth, B. (2007). ASSIST: adaptive social support for information space traversal, ACM Hypertext 2007. DOI: 10.1145/1286240.1286299

Felsenstein, J. (2002). Inferring Phylogenies, Sinauer Associates Inc., U.S., 2002.

Fountain, A.M., Hall, W., Heath, I., and Davis, H.C. (1990). MICROCOSM: An Open Model for Hypermedia with Dynamic Linking, ECHT '90, pp. 298–311.

Furuta, R. (1992). Important Papers in the History of Document Preparation Systems: Basic Sources. In Electronic Publishing: Origination, Dissemination & Design 5(1).

Furuta, R., Shipman III, F.M., Marshall, C.C., Brenner, D., and Hsieh, H. (1997). Hypertext paths and the World-Wide Web: experiences with Walden's Paths, April 1997, ACM Hypertext '97. DOI: 10.1145/267437.267455

Garzotto, F., Mainetti, L., and Paolini, P. (1994). Adding multimedia collections to the Dexter Model, September 1994, ACM ECHT '94. DOI: 10.1145/192757.192774

Garzotto, F., Mainetti, L., and Paolini, P. (1995). Hypermedia design, analysis, and evaluation issues, August 1995, Communications of the ACM, Volume 38 Issue 8. DOI: 10.1145/208344.208349

Garzotto, F., Paolini, P., and Schwabe, D. (1991). HDM—a model for the design of hypertext applications, September 1991, ACM Hypertext '91. DOI: 10.1145/122974.123004

Garzotto, F., Paolini, P., and Schwabe, D. (1993). HDM—a model-based approach to hypertext application design, January 1993, ACM Transactions on Information Systems (TOIS), Volume 11 Issue 1. DOI: 10.1145/151480.151483

Goldfarb, C. (1990). The SGML Handbook. Clarendon Press, Oxford.

Goldfarb, C. (1996). The Roots of SGML - A Personal Recollection.
http://www.sgmlsource.com/history/roots.htm.

Goldfarb, C.F. (1981). A generalized approach to document markup. In Proceedings of the ACM SIGPLAN SIGOA Symposium on Text Manipulation (Portland, Oregon, United States, June 08-10, 1981). ACM, New York, NY, 68–73. DOI: 10.1145/800209.806456

Grønbæk, K. (1994). Composites in a Dexter-based hypermedia framework, September 1994, ACM ECHT '94. DOI: 10.1145/192757.192771

Grønbæk, K. (2006). Ubiquitous hypermedia and social interaction in physical environments, ACM Hypertext 2006. DOI: 10.1145/1149941.1149965

Grønbæk, K. and Trigg, R.H. (1994a). Design issues for a Dexter-based hypermedia system, February 1994, Communications of the ACM, Volume 37 Issue 2. DOI: 10.1145/175235.175238

Grønbæk, K. and Trigg, R.H. (1996). Toward a Dexter-based model for open hypermedia: unifying embedded references and link objects, March 1996, ACM Hypertext '96. DOI: 10.1145/234828.234843

Grønbæk, K., and Trigg, R.H. (1994b). Hypermedia system design applying the Dexter model, February 1994, Communications of the ACM, Volume 37 Issue 2. DOI: 10.1145/175235.175236

Grønbæk, K., Bouvin, N.O., and Sloth, L. (1997). Designing Dexter-based hypermedia services for the World Wide Web, April 1997, ACM Hypertext '97. DOI: 10.1145/267437.267453

Guimarães, N. (1991). Building generic user interface tools: an experience with multiple inheritance, November 1991, ACM OOPSLA '91. DOI: 10.1145/118014.117961

Guimarães, N., Correia, N., and Carmo, T.A. (1992). Programming time in multimedia user interfaces, December 1992, ACM UIST '92. DOI: 10.1145/142621.142637

Haake, A. and Hicks, D. (1997). VerSE: Towards Hypertext Versioning Styles, ACM Hypertext' 97. DOI: 10.1145/234828.234850

Haake, J.M., Neuwirth, C.M., and Streitz, N. (1994). Coexistence and transformation of informal and formal structures: requirements for more flexible hypermedia systems, September 1994, ACM ECHT '94. DOI: 10.1145/192757.192758

Haan, B., Kahn, P., Riley, V., Coombs, J., and Meyrowitz, N. (1992). IRIS Hypermedia Services. Communications of the ACM, January 1992. DOI: 10.1145/129617.129618

Halasz, F. and Schwartz, M. (1994). The Dexter Hypertext Reference Model, Communications of the ACM, February 1994. DOI: 10.1145/175235.175237

Halasz, F.G. (1988). Reflections on NoteCards: Seven Issues for die Next Generation of Hypermedia Systems. Communications of the ACM, 31(7), July 1988. DOI: 10.1145/48511.48514

Halasz, F.G., Moran, T.P., and Trigg, R.H. (1987). NoteCards in a nutshell, April 1987, ACM CHI '87: SIGCHI/GI. DOI: 10.1145/30851.30859

Hall, B.G. (2007). Phylogenetic Trees Made Easy: A How-to Manual, Sinauer Associates Inc., 3rd ed., Aug 2007.

Hansen, F.A. and Grønbæk, K. (2008). Social web applications in the city: a lightweight infrastructure for urban computing, ACM Hypertext 2008. DOI: 10.1145/1379092.1379126

Hardman, L., Bulterman, D.C.A., and van Rossum, G. (1994). The Amsterdam hypermedia model: adding time and context to the Dexter model, Communications of the ACM, 37(2), February, 1994. DOI: 10.1145/175235.175239

Hardman, L., et al (1993). The Amsterdam Hypertext Model: extending hypertext to support real multimedia, Hypermedia Journal 5 (1), July 1993.

Harvey, G. (1988). Understanding HyperCard. Alameda, CA: SYBEX Inc., 1988.

Hendler, J., Shadbolt, N., Hall, W., Berners-Lee, T., and Weitzner, D. (2008). Web science: an interdisciplinary approach to understanding the web, July 2008, Communications of the ACM, Volume 51 Issue 7. DOI: 10.1145/1364782.1364798

Hill, G. and Hall, W. (1994). Extending the Microcosm Model to a Distributed Environment. ACM ECHT 1994: 32–40. DOI: 10.1145/192757.192763

Hirata, K., Hara, Y., Takano, H., and Kawasaki, S. (1996). Content Oriented Integration in Hypermedia Systems, ACM Hypertext 1996. DOI: 10.1145/234828.234830

Hodges, M.E., Sasnett, R.M., and Ackerman, M.S. (1989). A Construction Set for Multimedia Applications, IEEE Xplore, January 1989. DOI: 10.1109/52.16900

Holdener, A. (2008). Ajax: The Definitive Guide, O'Reilly Media, Inc., January 2008.

ISO (1986). Text and Office Systems—Standard Generalized Markup Language, October 1986. Document Number: ISO 8879–1986(E).

ISO (1989a). Text and Office Systems—Office Document Architecture, (ODA) and Interchange Format, International Standards Organization 1989. International Standard 8613.

ISO (1989b). ISO/IEC CD10179, Information Technology – Text and Office Systems - Document Style Semantics and Specification Language(DSSSL), 1991. International Standards Organization, ISO/IEC Draft International Standard 10179.

ISO (1997). Hypermedia/Time-based Structuring Language (HyTime), 2nd Edition, ISO/IEC JTC1/SC18/WG8 N1920 (1997-08-01).

Joyce, M., Kaplan, N., McDaid, J., and Moulthrop, S. (1989). Hypertext, narrative, and consciousness,November 1989, ACM Hypertext '89. DOI: 10.1145/74224.74254

Kahn, P., Launhaidt, J., Lenk, K., and Peters, R. (1990). Design of Hypermedia Publications: Issues and Solution. International Conference on Electronic Publishing, EP90, pp. 107–124, September 1990. Cambridge University Press.

Kaplan, N. and Moulthrop, S. (1994). Where no mind has gone before: ontological design for virtual spaces, September 1994, ACM ECHT '94. DOI: 10.1145/192757.192832

Kitching, I.J. (1998). Cladistics: Theory and Practice of Parsimony Analysis: The Theory and Practice of Parsimony Analysis, Oxford University Press, 1998.

Knuth, D.E. (1978). TEX: A System for Technical Text. Tech. Rept. AIM-217, Stanford University, November, 1978.

Kobsa A., Koenemann J., and Pohl, W. (2001). Personalised Hypermedia Presentation Techniques For Improving Online Customer Relationships. The Knowledge Engineering Review, Vol. 16:2, 111–155. Cambridge University Press, 2001. DOI: 10.1017/S0269888901000108

Koved, L. and Shneiderman, B. (1986). Embedded menus: Selecting items in context, Communications of the ACM 29, 4 (April 1986), 312–318. DOI: 10.1145/5684.5687

Krottmaier, H. (2002). Aspects of Modern Electronic Publishing Systems, Ph.D. Thesis, Graz University of Technology, December 2002.
`http://fiicm2pc43.tu-graz.ac.at/Teaching/theses/2002/_idb70_/`
`hkrott_diss.pdf`.

Lamport, L. (1994). LaTeX: A document preparation system. Addison-Wesley Professional.

Landow, G.P. (1987). Relationally Encoded Links and the Rhetoric of Hypertext, ACM Hypertext '87, pp. 331–344, 1987. DOI: 10.1145/317426.317450

Landow, G.P. (1994). Hyper/Text/Theory. Johns Hopkins Press, 1994.

Leggett, J.J. and Schnase, J.L. (1994). Viewing Dexter with open eyes. Communications of the ACM 37, 2 (Feb. 1994), 76–86. DOI: 10.1145/175235.175241

Lerner, F. (1998). The Story of Libraries: From the Invention of Writing to the Computer Age, Continuum International Publishing Group Ltd., illustrated edition, December 1998.

Lévy, P. (1990). Les Technologies de l'intelligence, Ed. La Decouverte, 1990.

Lewis, P.H., Davis, H.C., Griffiths, S., Hall, W., and Wilkins, R. (1996). Media-based Navigation with Generic Links. Hypertext 1996: 215–223. DOI: 10.1145/234828.234849

Madison, D.R., Swofford, D.L., and Maddison, W.P. (1997). Nexus: an extensible file format for systematic information, Systematic Biology, Dec 1997, 46(4):590–621. DOI: 10.2307/2413497

Mark, G., Haake, J.M., and Streitz, N. (1996). Hypermedia structures and the division of labor in meeting room collaboration, November 1996, ACM CSCW '96. DOI: 10.1145/240080.240247

Marshall, C.C., Halasz, F.G., Rogers, R., and Janssen, W. (1991). Aquanet: A Hypertext Tool to Hold Your Knowledge in Place, ACM Hypertext '91. DOI: 10.1145/122974.123000

Marshall, C.C. and Irish, P.M. (1989). Guided tours and on-line presentations: how authors make existing hypertext intelligible for readers, November 1989, ACM Hypertext '89. DOI: 10.1145/74224.74226

Maturana, H. and Varela, F. (1987). The Tree of Knowledge – The Biological Roots of Human Understanding, Shambhala, 1987.

Maurer, H. (1995). The Graz digital library effort, September 1995, SIGWEB Newsletter, Volume 4 Issue 2.

McCracken, D.L. and Akscyn, R.M. (1984). Experience with the ZOG human-computer interface system, October 1984, International Journal of Man-Machine Studies, Volume 21 Issue 4. DOI: 10.1016/S0020-7373(84)80050-4

Mertens, R., Farzan, R., and Brusilovsky, P. (2006). Social navigation in web lectures, ACM Hypertext 2006. DOI: 10.1145/1149941.1149950

Meyrowitz, N. (1986). Intermedia : The Architecture and Construction of an Object-Oriented Hypermedia System and Applications Framework. ACM OOPSLA'86, pp. 186–201, September 1986.
DOI: 10.1145/960112.28716

Meyrowitz, N. and van Dam, A. (1982). Interactive Editing Systems: Part II, September 1982, Computing Surveys (CSUR), Volume 14 Issue 3.

Michel, S.L. (1988). HyperCard – The Complete Reference. Osborne McGraw-Hill, 1988.

Mitchell, M. (1998). An Introduction to Genetic Algorithms, MIT Press, 1998.

Moulthrop, S. (1991). Beyond the electronic book: a critique of hypertext rhetoric, September 1991, ACM Hypertext '91. DOI: 10.1145/122974.123001

Moulthrop, S. (1992). Toward a rhetoric of informating texts, December 1992, ACM ECHT '92. DOI: 10.1145/168466.168520

Natchez, M. and Prose, T. (1989). Creating effective Hypercard online documentation and training, November 1989, SIGDOC '89: Proceedings of the 7th annual international conference on Systems Documentation. DOI: 10.1145/74311.74318

Nelson, T.H. (1980). Literary Machines. Mindful Press, Sausalito, California, 1980.

Nelson, T.H. (1995). The heart of connection: hypermedia unified by transclusion, August 1995, Communications of the ACM, Volume 38 Issue 8. DOI: 10.1145/208344.208353

Nelson, T.H. (1999). The unfinished revolution and Xanadu™, December 1999, Computing Surveys (CSUR), Volume 31, Issue 4.

Neuwirth, C. and Ogura, A. (1988). The Andrew System Programmer's Guide to the Andrew Toolkit, CMU-ITC TR, Carnegie-Mellon University, November 1986. http://reports-archive.adm.cs.cmu.edu/itc85.html.

Newcomb, S.R., Kipp, N.A., and Newcomb, V.T. (1991). The "HyTime ": hypermedia/time-based document structuring language, November 1991, Communications of the ACM, Volume 34 Issue 11. DOI: 10.1145/125490.125495

Nielsen, J. (1990). The art of navigating through hypertext, March 1990, Communications of the ACM, Volume 33 Issue 3. DOI: 10.1145/77481.77483

Nuernberg, P., Leggett, J., and Wiil, U. (1998). An Agenda for Open Hypermedia Research, ACM Hypertext'98. DOI: 10.1145/276627.276649

Oliveira, M., Turine, M., and Masiero, P. (2001). A Statechart-Based Model for Hypermedia Applications, ACM Transactions on IS, Jan 2001. DOI: 10.1145/366836.366869

Page, R.D.M. and Homes, E.C. (1998). Molecular Evolution: A Phylogenetic Approach, WileyBlackwell, 1998.

Palay, A.J., et al (1988). CMU-ITC-061, The Andrew Toolkit - An Overview, 1988.

Paulo, O.S., Pinheiro, J., Miraldo, A., Bruford, W., Jordan, W.C., and Nichols, R.A. (2008). The role of vicariance vs. dispersal in shaping genetic patterns in ocellated lizard species in the western Mediterranean, Molecular Ecology (2008) **17**, 1535–1551. http://10.1111/j.1365-294X.2008.03706.x. DOI: 10.1111/j.1365-294X.2008.03706.x

Pearl, A. (1989). Sun's Link Service: a protocol for open linking, November 1989, ACM Hypertext '89. DOI: 10.1145/74224.74236

Purves, W.K., Sadava, D., Orians, G.H., and Heller, C. (2004). Life, the Science of Biology, 7th ed., Sinauer Associates, 2004.

Puttress, J. and Guimarães, N. (1990). The Toolkit Approach to Hypermedia, Hypertext: concepts, systems and applications, European Conference on Hypertext, ECHT'90, November 1990, Cambrige University Press.

Rapaport, D. (1974). The History of the Concept of Association of Ideas, International Universities Press, 1974.

Reid, B.K. (1980). A high-level approach to computer document formatting. In Proceedings of the 7th ACM SIGPLAN-SIGACT Symposium on Principles of Programming Languages (Las Vegas, Nevada, January 28 - 30, 1980). POPL '80. ACM, New York, NY, 24–31. DOI: 10.1145/567446.567449

Roisin, C. (1998). Authoring Structured Multimedia Documents. In SOFSEM' 98: Theory and Practice of Informatics, pp. 222–239, Volume 1521/1998, Springer. DOI: 10.1007/3-540-49477-4_15

Romero, L. and Correia, N. (2003). HyperReal: a hypermedia model for mixed reality, August 2003, ACM Hypertext'03. DOI: 10.1145/900051.900055

Rossi, G., Lyardet, F.D., and Schwabe D. (1999). Developing hypermedia applications with methods and patterns, December 1999, ACM Computing Surveys, Volume 31 Issue 4. DOI: 10.1145/345966.345987

Saitou, N. and Nei, M. (1987). The neighbor-joining method: A new method for reconstructing phylogenetic trees. *Molecular Biology and Evolution* 4: 406–425.

Salemi, M. and Vandamme A.-M. (2003). The Phylogenetic Handbook: A Practical Approach to DNA and Protein Phylogeny, Cambridge University Press, 2003.

Sauer, S. and Engels, G. (2001). UML-based Behavior Specification of Interactive Multimedia Applications. HCC '01, IEEE Symposia on Human-Centric Computing Languages and Environments, September 2001. DOI: 10.1109/HCC.2001.995271

Sawhney, N., Balcom, D., and Smith, I. (1996). HyperCafe: narrative and aesthetic properties of hypervideo, March 1996, ACM Hypertext '96. DOI: 10.1145/234828.234829

Schütt, H.A. and Streitz, N.A. (1990). HyperBase: a hypermedia engine based on a relational database management system, Hypertext: concepts, systems and applications, European Conference on Hypertext, ECHT'90, November 1990, Cambrige University Press.

Schwabe, D., Rossi G., and Barbosa, S.D.J. (1996). Systematic hypermedia application design with OOHDM, March 1996, ACM Hypertext '96. DOI: 10.1145/234828.234840

Schwabe, D. and Rossi, G. (1995). The object-oriented hypermedia design model, August 1995, Communications of the ACM, Volume 38 Issue 8. DOI: 10.1145/208344.208354

Segaran, T., Evans, C., and Taylor, J. (2009). Programming the Semantic Web, O'Reilly Media, Inc, July 2009.

Sherman, M., Hansen, W.J., McInerny, M., and Neuendorffer, T. (1990). CMU-ITC-090, Building Hypertexty on a Multimedia Toolkit: An Overview of Andrew Toolkit Hypermedia Facilities, August 1990.

Shneiderman, B. (1987). User interface design for the Hyperties electronic encyclopedia, Hypertext '87 Workshop Proceedings, Raleigh, NC, November 13-15, 1987, 199–204. DOI: 10.1145/317426.317441

Shneiderman, B. (1988a). Designing the User Interface: Strategies for Effective Human Computer Interaction, Addison Wesley, 3rd ed., 1998.

Shneiderman, B. (1989). Reflections on authoring, editing, and managing hypertext. In Barrett, E. (Editor), *The Society of Text*, MIT Press, Cambridge, MA (1989), 115–131.

Shneiderman, B., Ed. (1988b). *Hypertext on Hypertext*, Hyperties disk with 1Mbyte data and graphics incorporating Communication of the ACM (July 1988), New York: ACM Press.

Simpson, R., Renear, A., Mylonas, E., and van Dam, A. (1996). 50 Years after "As We May Think": the Brown/MIT Vannevar Bush Symposium", Interactions, Mar 1996. DOI: 10.1145/227181.227187

Stevenson, D., Ed. (1998). Cladistics, Journal, Published on behalf of the Willi Hennig Society, Wiley Blackwell.

Stotts, P. and Furuta, R. (1989). Petri-Net-Based Hypertext: Document Structure with Browsing Semantics, ACM Transactions on IS, Jan 1989. DOI: 10.1145/64789.64791

Streitz, N.A., Hannemann, J., and Thüring, M. (1989). From ideas and arguments to hyperdocuments: travelling through activity spaces, November 1989, ACM Hypertext '89. DOI: 10.1145/74224.74251

Streitz, N., Geißler, J., Haake, J.M., and Hol, J. (1994). DOLPHIN: integrated meeting support across local and remote desktop environments and LiveBoards, October 1994, ACM CSCW '94. DOI: 10.1145/192844.193044

Streitz, N., Haake, J., Hannemann, J., Lemke, A., Schuler, W., Schütt, H., and Thüring, M. (1993). SEPIA: a cooperative hypermedia authoring environment, December 1993, ACM ECHT '92. DOI: 10.1145/168466.168479

Thüring, M., Hannemann J., and Haake, J.M. (1995). Hypermedia and cognition: designing for comprehension, August 1995, Communications of the ACM, Volume 38 Issue 8. DOI: 10.1145/208344.208348

Tompa, F. (1989). A Data Model for Flexible Hypertext Systems, ACM Transactions on IS, Jan 1989. DOI: 10.1145/64789.64993

Toulmin, S.E. (2003). The Uses of Argument, Cambridge University Press,(updated edition), 2003.

Trigg, R.H., Suchman, L.A., and Halasz, F.G. (1986). Supporting collaboration in notecards, December 1986, ACM CSCW '86. DOI: 10.1145/637069.637089

W3C (1999). HTML 4.01 Specification, W3C Recommendation, December 1999. http://www.w3.org/TR/html401.

W3C (2001). XML Linking Language (XLink) Version 1.0. W3C Recommendation, June 2001. http://www.w3.org/TR/xlink.

W3C (2006). Extensible Markup Language (XML) 1.1 (Second Edition), W3C Recommendation, September 2006. http://www.w3.org/TR/2006/REC-xml11-20060816.

W3C (2008). Synchronized Multimedia Integration Language (SMIL 3.0), W3C Recommendation, December 2008. http://www.w3.org/TR/SMIL3.

W3C (2009a), Cascading Style Sheets Level 2 Revision 1 (CSS 2.1) Specification, W3C Candidate Recommendation, April 2009. http://www.w3.org/TR/CSS2.

W3C (2009b). The Extensible Stylesheet Language Family (XSL). http://www.w3.org/Style/XSL.

Wang, W. and Rada, R. (1998). Structured hypertext with domain semantics, October 1998, Transactions on Information Systems (TOIS), Volume 16 Issue 4.

Wang, W. and Rubart, J. (2006). A cognitive and social framework for shared understanding in cooperative hypermedia authoring, ACM Hypertext 2006. DOI: 10.1145/1149941.1149953

Wiil, U. and Leggett, J. (1996). The Hyperdisco Approach to Open Hypermedia Systems, Hypertext'96. DOI: 10.1145/234828.234842

Winograd, T. and Flores, F. (1986). Understanding Computers and Cognition – A New Foundation for Design, Addison Wesley, 1986.

Yankelovitch, N., Hanna, B.J., Meyrowitz, N., and Drucker S. (1989). Intermedia The Concept and the Construction of a Seamless Information Environment. IEEE Computer, 21(1):81–96, January 1989. DOI: 10.1109/2.222120

Yoder, E., Akscyn, R.M., and McCracken, D.L. (1989). Collaboration in KMS, a shared hypermedia system, March 1989, CHI '89. DOI: 10.1145/67449.67457

Zellweger, P.T. (1989). Scripted documents: a hypermedia path mechanism, November 1989, ACM Hypertext '89. DOI: 10.1145/74224.74225

Authors' Biographies

NUNO GUIMARÃES

Nuno Guimarães graduated in Electrical Engineering at the Technical University of Lisbon, Instituto Superior Técnico (School of Engineering), Portugal, in 1983, where he pursued postgraduate studies (MSc and PhD in Computer and Electrical Engineering). He is currently Full Professor at the Computer Science (Informatics) at the Faculty of Sciences of the University of Lisbon. From 2004 to 2009, he was Dean of the Faculty of Sciences of the University of Lisbon. From 1982 to 1997, he was a researcher of INESC, Instituto de Engenharia de Sistemas e Computadores, Lisbon, Portugal. Since 1990, he was responsible for the "Multimedia and Interaction Techniques" Group, and participated in technical developments and coordination of national and international projects. Between 1989 and 1991, he was a consultant for Bell Labs, AT&T, Murray Hill, New Jersey, "Software Systems Principles Research Lab," working in the areas of User Interfaces and early experiences with Hypertext Systems. From 1996 to 2002, he co-founded several start up companies operating in the areas of Multimedia, Workflow, and Collaborative Computing. He is a Senior Member of ACM.

LUÍS CARRIÇO

Luís Carriço is an Associate Professor at the University of Lisbon's Department of Computer Science (Informatics). His main research interests have addressed Human Computer Interaction, User Centred Design, Mobile Interface Design, Pervasive Computing, Hypermedia, Groupware, Accessibility, and Ehealth. He received his PhD (2000) in Electrical and Computer Engineering from the Technical University of Lisbon. He has published more than one hundred articles in journals, books, and conferences, and participated in more than eighteen research and development projects, six of which international. He was a member of more than fifty program committees and he is an invited reviewer and evaluator for the European Commission. He is the leader of the AbsInt (Absolute Interaction) team, at the HCIM (Human Computer Interaction and Multimedia) Group, and a senior researcher at LaSIGE (Large Scale Informatics Systems) research unit.